Creamy Red Pepper Soup (page 51)

About The Author

Lou Seibert Pappas is the food editor of the Peninsula Times Tribune in Palo Alto, California. A former food consultant for "Sunset Magazine," she now writes for "Gourmet" and "Cuisine" magazines and is the author of a dozen other cookbooks, including **Favorite Cookie Recipes, Extra-Special Crockery Pot Recipes** and **Bread Baking.** She has made 10 extensive trips to Europe collecting recipes and ideas for her books and taking photographs.

A fresh and creative soup and salad recipe for every occasion

- Whether the interest is in stylish entertaining or a dinner for one, this cookbook has it.

- Ideas for everything from luscious California salads to tempting artichoke heart soup.

- Special tips for using the food processor.

- Nutrition-conscious cooks will welcome the use of seasonal produce and of preparation ideas for keeping salt and fats to a minimum.

- For easy use, this book lies flat when opened, contains one recipe per page and is printed in large easy-to-read type.

- Compact design—takes a minimum of counter space.

Creative
Soups & Salads

by Lou Seibert Pappas

©Copyright 1983
Nitty Gritty Productions
P.O. Box 5457
Concord, California 94524-0457

A Nitty Gritty Cookbook
Printed by Mariposa Press
Concord, California

ISBN 0-911954-81-3
Library of Congress Catalog Card Number 83-061789

First Edition

Editor: Jackie Walsh
Art Director: Mike Nelson
Photographer: Glen Millward
Food Stylist: Bobbie Greenlaw

Special thanks to **Candlelight Gifts**
(Walnut Creek, CA) and to
Fair & Warmer (Walnut Creek, CA)
for the cookware and props
in our photographs.

Table of Contents

Soups

Salads

Introduction

A bubbling pot of aromatic soup is one of life's great comforting pleasures. Healthy, delicious, easy and economical, soups are a natural for dining. At both informal and elegant occasions, they add a special flair.

Soups come in countless flavors and variations. However they easily divide into several categories. Refreshing frosty cold soups are ideal for brunch, a summer luncheon starter or dessert finale. First course or appetizer soups make great treats to pass in small cups or glasses in the garden or living room as a prelude to dinner. Full-meal soups may star as the main entree at lunch or preside in the evening at dinner or late supper. Vegetable soups make fine luncheon dishes with a salad bar or served as a separate course at a meal.

Warming, nourishing and brimming with endless variety, soups let the cook be imaginative and innovative. With a simmering stock the cook can be flexible, adding an extra vegetable to the pot for super flavor or substituting a celery stalk and an onion for hard-to-find leeks. Soups stretch and expand with ease to satisfy an unexpected guest at the table.

Toppings and condiments for soup offer many possibilities. Often they turn a soup supper into a memorable meal as guests decorate their bowls with color and flavor. Shredded cheese, chives, green onions, sunflower seeds, toasted almonds roasted cashews or pistachios, shredded hard-cooked egg, sour cream, yogurt, whipped cream, caviar, chopped apple, small cooked shrimp and diced avocado make fine additions for appropriate soups.

Today the food processor and the blender simplify soup making. The ingredients can be easily chopped or grated with a food processor to shorten the time involved. At the end of the simmering time, either machine can whisk a chunky melange into a smooth puree. If you want some texture left in your soup a food processor works well. Remember to let the soup cool slightly before blending it. Very hot soup can raise the lid of the processor or blender and the soup may spew out of the container.

Basic stocks are easy to make and greatly enhance a soup. Just collect extra chicken necks, backs and wings in your freezer. Also ask your butcher for beef or veal bones. Wrap and freeze any bones left from boning chicken breasts or from leftover roasts of chicken, lamb, beef or pork. When you have good supply make a big batch of stock at one time. If you have large pots and pans, make great quantitites of stock. Cooking 3 pounds of bones takes as much time as cooking 20 pounds of bones. You can even give some of your frozen, homemade stock to less fortunate friends as gifts.

Remember that stock expands considerably when frozen, so allow extra room in the container. Extra milk cartons, plastic containers or wide-mouth jars make good containers to hold stock in the freezer. Make sure they are airtight so the stock does not pick up flavors from the freezer.

Do not salt any of the **basic stocks.** This eliminates the possibility of over-salting when you combine the stock with other ingredients for a soup.

A stock must cook a certain amount of time, which varies depending on how large the bones are and what bones are used. Thin, small bones such as fish and chicken will be finished in 3 hours of cooking. Large veal and beef bones require up to 10 or 12 hours. You may cook your stock over several days, just bring it to a boil each day and then reduce to a steady simmer. During cooking the water gradually evaporates. Add more to keep the bones well-covered.

If your time is scarce and no homemade stock is at hand, use canned soup stocks, bouillon cubes or crystals.

The easiest way to remove surplus fat from a soup stock or prepared soup is to chill the soup. The fat will solidify on the top and can easily be lifted off.

The following basic stocks are essential for the soup cook. Keep them handy in the freezer, ready for instant use.

Basic Beef Stock

Mix veal, beef and chicken bones for a pleasant, nutty flavor. Ask your butcher for a few beef and veal bones or buy shanks or knuckles.

4 lbs. beef, veal and chicken bones
4 qts. cold water
1 onion stuck with 6 cloves
2 stalks celery, chopped
1 carrot, coarsely chopped

6 sprigs parsley
1/2 tsp. thyme
1 bay leaf
1/4 tsp. black peppercorns

In a large sauce pan put bones in one layer. Cook on high heat to brown. Reduce heat to medium and cook, stirring often, until very brown but not burned, about 25 minutes. Cover with cold water. Slowly bring to a boil. Remove scum. Add onion, celery, carrot, parsley, thyme, bay leaf and pepper. Simmer steadily for 10 to 12 hours. Strain. Cool. Refrigerate. Lift off fat. Use within 2 to 3 days or freeze. Makes about 2 quarts. Recipe may be doubled.

Basic Chicken Stock

Make in quantity and freeze in portions that match the amounts required in your favorite recipes.

4 lbs. chicken bones, necks, backs and wings
4 qts. cold water
1 onion, stuck with 4 cloves
2 carrots, coarsely chopped
1 stalk celery, chopped

4 sprigs parsley
1 bay leaf
1/2 tsp. thyme
1/4 tsp. black peppercorns

In a large saucepan place the chicken bones and water. Bring to a boil. Remove any scum. Add onion, carrot, celery, parsley, bay leaf, thyme and pepper. Simmer 2 to 3 hours. Strain. Cool. Refrigerate. Lift off fat. Use within 2 to 3 days or freeze. You may also freeze at once after cooking. Makes about 2 quarts. Recipe may be doubled.

Fish Stock

Ask for fish bones at the fish counter. Avoid strong-flavored fish such as mullet or salmon.

2 lbs. washed fish bones, heads, tails
   and trimmings
1 small onion, chopped
1 inner stalk celery, chopped
1/2 cup chopped carrot
2 tbs. butter

1/2 cup dry white wine
4 cups water
1 bay leaf
few sprigs parsley
1/2 tsp. thyme
1/4 tsp. black peppercorns

In a large saucepan saute onion, celery and carrot in butter until limp. Add wine, water, bay leaf, parsley, thyme, pepper, fish bones and trimmings. Bring to boil. Simmer over medium-high heat, uncovered, for 20 minutes. Strain. Let cool. Refrigerate. Use within 2 days or freeze. Makes about 2 cups. Recipe may be doubled.

Quick and Easy Appetizer Soups

A refreshing starter to an informal meal is a light soup attractively served in small mugs, Chinese tea cups or wine glasses. Arranged on a tray, soup served in this manner is ideal to pass in the living room or garden to almost any number of guests. Sipping a flavorful soup sets a relaxed and friendly tone for the meal that follows.

All of the soups in this section can also be served at the table as a first course for a delightful beginning to almost any meal, be it brunch, lunch, dinner or a light supper.

Most of these light soups can be made in advance—and they do go together quickly—ready to reheat at the last minute. Their flavor spectrum ranges from a piquant wine-laced Austrian soup to a cheese-enriched Italian soup.

Pairing these first course soups with a complementary salad makes an extra-special meal. Consider serving Orange-Zested Spicy Broth with Summer Beef Salad (page 154), Vintner's Broth with Pesto and the Bistro Salad (page 136) or Parador Soup with Salade Nicoise (page 164). There are many other wonderful combinations possible using the recipes in this book.

Preparation time: 15 minutes
Cooking time: 10 minutes
Servings: 4

Greek Lemon Soup

3 cups chicken stock (homemade preferred)
3 eggs
1/4 cup fresh lemon juice
4 lemon slices for garnish
few sprigs fresh dill **or** parsley (optional garnish)

Using a large saucepot, heat chicken stock to boiling. In a medium bowl beat eggs until blended. Add lemon juice. Gradually pour half the hot stock into the egg-lemon mixture, beating with a whisk as you pour. Return to saucepot with remaining stock and heat over low heat, stirring until thickened. **Do not boil.** Ladle into soup bowls or wine glasses. Float a lemon slice on each and garnish with dill or parsley.

FLUFFY VARIATION: Use ingredients as listed above except separate eggs. Place yolks and whites in separate medium-size bowls. Beat yolks with lemon juice until blended. Beat whites until soft peaks form. Fold whites into yolk-lemon mixture. Gradually beat in half the hot stock. Return to saucepot with remaining stock. Cook over low heat, stirring, until thickened.

Preparation time: 15 minutes
Cooking time: 10 minutes
Servings: 2 to 3

Creamy Chicken Broth Supreme

Here is a fast, elegant appetizer when dinner guests arrive unexpectedly.

1 shallot **or** 2 green onions, chopped
1 tsp. butter
2-1/2 cups chicken stock
1/4 cup slivered Danish ham **or** crab meat
2 egg yolks
2 tsp. lemon juice
freshly ground nutmeg, about 1/8 tsp.
2 tsp. chopped parsley

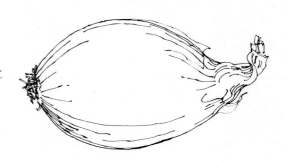

In a saucepan saute the shallot or onions in butter until limp. Add the stock and ham. Heat until boiling. In a small bowl beat egg yolks until light. Beat in the lemon juice. Gradually stir in about 1/3 cup of the hot stock. Beating constantly, slowly add egg-lemon mixture to soup. Cook over very low heat, stirring, until thickened. **Do not boil.** Ladle into bowls. Sprinkle with nutmeg and parsley.

Preparation time: 10 minutes
Cooking time: 10 minutes
Servings: 6

Maritata Soup

This elegant, creamy-rich Italian soup can be sipped from small cups or mugs in the garden or living room.

1/3 cup unsalted butter, at room temperature
1/2 cup grated Monterey Jack **or** Fontina cheese
1/4 cup grated Romano **or** Parmesan cheese
3 egg yolks
3/4 cup whipping cream
3-1/2 cups chicken stock
3/4 cup dry white wine
minced parsley for garnish

In a mixing bowl beat together butter, cheeses and egg yolks. Gradually mix in the cream. In a large saucepan, heat chicken stock and wine to boiling. Mix a little hot stock into the creamy-cheese mixture, stirring contantly. Stir into the remaining stock in the pan. Heat and ladle into small cups or wine glasses for easy sipping. Sprinkle with parsley.

Austrian Wine Soup

Serve this with a glass of white wine and let guests lace their soup with a bit of the wine as they do in Austria.

2 tbs. butter
2 green onions, chopped
2 tbs. chopped chives
2 tbs. flour
2-1/2 cups chicken stock

3/4 cup dry white wine
3 egg yolks
1/3 cup whipping cream
dash freshly grated nutmeg
salt and pepper to taste

Melt butter in a saucepan. Saute onions and chives 1 minute. Add flour and saute 2 minutes, stirring. Add stock and wine. Bring to a boil. In a small bowl beat egg yolks until light and mix in cream. Stir part of the hot stock into the egg mixture. Return to the remaining stock in the saucepan. Cook, stirring until thickened. Do not let boil. Season with nutmeg, salt and pepper to taste.

Preparation time: 5 minutes
Cooking time: 10 minutes
Servings: 4

Stracciatella

This simple Italian soup goes together quickly. Fresh basil is best and is easy to grow in the summer. Many markets also carry fresh basil when it is in season.

2 cups chicken stock
2 tbs. dry white wine
1 egg
3 tbs. grated Romano **or** Parmesan cheese
1 tbs. minced parsley
1 tbs. chopped fresh basil **or** 3/4 tsp. dried basil

In a large saucepan heat stock and wine to boiling. In a small mixing bowl beat the egg with cheese, parsley and basil. Pour egg mixture into boiling stock and remove pan from heat; **do not stir.** Ladle into small cups or glasses.

Preparation time: 5 minutes
Cooking time: 10 minutes
Servings: 4 to 6

Parador Soup

This Latin soup goes together in a flourish.

1 qt. chicken stock
few drops Tabasco
1/2 cup slivered chicken **or** ham
2 green onions, chopped
1 tomato, peeled, seeded and chopped
1 small red **or** green pepper, chopped
1/3 cup chopped cilantro
1 avocado, peeled and diced
tortilla chips for accompaniment

In a large saucepan or soup pot heat stock and Tabasco to boiling. Simmer 5 minutes. Add chicken or ham, onions, tomato and pepper. Remove from heat. Stir in cilantro and avocado. Ladle into bowls. Accompany with tortilla chips.

Creamy Corn Soup (page 50) ▶

Preparation time: 5 minutes
Cooking time: 10 minutes
Servings: 4

African Peanut Soup

This makes a novel prelude to an ethnic meal.

2 tbs. butter
4 green onions, chopped
2 tbs. flour
3 cups fish stock **or** chicken stock
1/2 tsp. chili powder
small dried red chili, crushed
3/4 cup roasted peanuts
1-1/2 cups finely shredded spinach leaves
cilantro sprigs for garnish

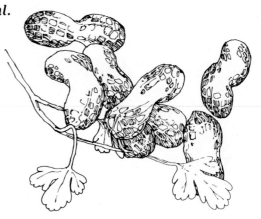

Melt butter in a large saucepan. Saute green onions and garlic until limp. Stir in 1 tablespoon flour and cook 2 minutes. Add fish stock, chili powder and chili. Bring to a boil. Grind peanuts with remaining flour in food processor or blender until medium fine. Add to the stock. Bring to a boil and simmer 5 minutes. Add spinach and simmer 1 minute longer. Ladle into small bowls and garnish with cilantro.

Preparation time: 5 minutes
Cooking time: 15 minutes
Servings: 4

Orange-Zested Spicy Broth

Use a vegetable peeler to cut the orange rind into thin slivers for this delightful low-calorie broth.

2 cups homemade beef stock
1/2 cup orange juice
1 cinnamon stick
2 cardamom seeds, shells removed
4 whole cloves **or** allspice
2 strips orange rind

In a saucepan combine the stock, orange juice, cinnamon stick, cardamom seeds and cloves. Bring to a boil. Simmer 10 to 15 minutes to develop flavors. Slice orange rind into fine strips, about 1/16-inch wide and 1/2-inch long. Add to soup. Ladle into cups.

Preparation time: 5 minutes
Cooking time: 10 minutes
Servings: 6

Vintner's Broth with Pesto

A dollop of pesto brings alive this wine-laced soup for a light and refreshing starter.

Pesto: see below
4 cups beef stock
1/2 cup dry red wine

First prepare Pesto. Heat stock and wine to serving temperature. Pour into small cups and top with Pesto.

PESTO: Place in a food processor or blender 1/3 cup grated Parmesan **or** Romano cheese, 3 tablespoons pine nuts **or** blanched almonds, 1 clove garlic, 1/4 cup chopped basil and 1 tablespoon butter. Process until blended.

Light and Refreshing Cold Soups

Cold soup is especially welcome for warmer days, and is a refreshing choice to begin a decorative luncheon or a barbecue-style dinner.

A variety of fresh produce, both fruits and vegetables, is adaptable to this style of soup. The colors are vivid, from the scarlet Garden Gazpacho to the creamy, pale green Curried Avocado Soup. And, the flavors range from savory vegetable to sweet fruit as in It's the Berries Soup or Cold Nectarine Soup.

It is best to make these soups in advance so they are well-chilled and the flavors have a chance to mellow. Then simply ladle them into pretty bowls and serve.

Preparation time: 10 minutes
Cooking time: 10 minutes
Servings: 4

Cold Nectarine Soup

This lightly-spiced fruity soup makes a fine starter for a summer picnic.

4 ripe nectarines
2 cups dry white wine
1 cup water
3 tbs. sugar
1 sliver fresh ginger root
2 whole cloves
lime slices for garnish

Peel nectarines, halve and remove pits. Thinly slice. Place in a saucepan (not aluminum) with wine, water, sugar, ginger root and cloves. Bring to a boil. Cover and simmer 10 minutes. Remove cloves. Let nectarine mixture cool slightly. Puree in a food processor or blender. Refrigerate at least 4 hours. Serve in wine goblets or other clear glasses, or chilled bowls, garnished with thin slices of lime.

Preparation time: 10 minutes
Cooking time: 10 minutes
Servings: 4

Strawberry Wine Soup

Here's a perfect ending for a summer meal—be it any time of day.

3 cups strawberries, hulled
1-1/2 cups fruity white wine
1/3 cup sugar
2 tbs. **each** cornstarch and cold water, mixed into a paste
2 tbs. amaretto liqueur **or** cassis syrup
whipped cream **or** sour cream for topping

Place berries, wine and sugar in saucepan. Bring to a boil. Simmer 5 minutes. Add cornstarch paste and cook until thickened. Let cool slightly, then puree in food processor or blender. Stir in liqueur or syrup. Refrigerate until chilled. Ladle into wine glasses or dessert bowls. Top with whipped or sour cream.

Preparation time: 10 minutes
Cooking time: 10 minutes
Servings: 4

It's The Berries Soup

This delectible Swedish-style soup is really an elegant dessert.

2 cups strawberries
1 cup raspberries
1/4 cup sugar
1 tbs. cornstarch

1/2 cup cold water
3 tbs. cassis syrup **or** liqueur of your choice
1/2 tsp. grated lemon peel
Whipped Cream Topping: see below

Hull and halve the strawberries. Place the strawberries, raspberries and sugar in a saucepan. Let stand 15 minutes for juices to exude. Heat over low heat to boiling. Mix together the cornstarch and water in a small bowl. Stir into berry mixture. Stirring constantly, bring mixture to a boil. Simmer until the fruit softens and the soup is clear and thickened, about 3 minutes. Remove from heat. Stir in cassis syrup or other liqueur and lemon peel. Refrigerate until cold, about 2 hours. To serve, spoon into dessert bowls and top with Whipped Cream Topping.
WHIPPED CREAM TOPPING: Whip 1/2 cup heavy cream until soft peaks form. Stir in 1 tablespoon amaretto liqueur **or** liqueur of your choice and 1 teaspoon sugar.

It's the Berries Soup (page 30) ▶

Preparation time: 5 minutes
Cooking time: 15 minutes
Servings: 6

Cranberry-Apple Soup

This ruby soup is festive for a holiday dinner first course. Or with cranberries available from the freezer, let it star on a picnic outing with a terrine, cheese and crudites.

1 package (12 ozs.) whole cranberries
2 cooking apples, peeled and diced
1/2 cup sugar
1-1/2 cups orange juice
1/2 cup water
1 tsp. grated orange peel
1 tsp. **each** cornstarch and cold water
sour cream for topping

Place cranberries, apple, sugar, orange juice, water and orange peel in a large saucepan. Bring to a boil. Cover and simmer 10 minutes, or until fruit is tender. Stir in a paste of the cornstarch and water. Cook until thickened. Let cool slightly. Puree in blender or food processor. Refrigerate until chilled. Ladle into bowls and top with sour cream.

Preparation time: 5 minutes
Cooking time: 5 minutes
Servings: 4

Curried Avocado Soup

1/2 tsp. curry powder
1 green onion, white part only, chopped
1 tsp. butter
1 large ripe avocado, peeled and pitted
1-1/2 cups chicken stock
2 tbs. light rum **or** 1/4 cup dry white wine
1 cup half-and-half **or** heavy cream
salt and pepper to taste
fresh chopped chives **or** sliced lime **or** lemon for garnish

In a small skillet, saute curry powder and onion in butter for 2 minutes. In food processor or blender puree the curry mixture, avocado, chicken stock, rum or wine and half-and-half. Season with salt and pepper to taste. Serve at once in well-chilled bowls, garnished with chives or lime or lemon slices.

Preparation time: 15 minutes
Cooking time: 30 minutes
Servings: 6

Cold Zucchini Soup

1 qt. shredded zucchini
salt
1 qt. chicken stock
3 green onions, chopped
2 cloves garlic, minced
1 tbs. fresh chopped basil **or** 3/4 teaspoon dried basil
salt and pepper to taste
2 tbs. quick-cooking farina (Cream of Wheat)
1/2 cup sour cream **or** whipping cream
chopped fresh basil **or** green onion tops for garnish

Place shredded zucchini in a colander. Sprinkle with salt. Let stand 15 minutes. Squeeze out liquid. In a large saucepan or souppot, place the zucchini, stock, onions, garlic, basil, salt and pepper. Bring to a boil. Stir in Cream of Wheat. Simmer 10 to 15 minutes. Let cool slightly. Puree in a food processor or blender. Blend in sour cream. Refrigerate until chilled. Serve in mugs or wine glasses. Garnish with chopped basil or onion tops.

Preparation time: 5 minutes
Cooking time: 10 minutes
Servings: 6

Minted Pea Soup

Fresh mint from the garden enlivens this pretty green soup.

2 packages (10 ozs. each) frozen tiny peas
3 cups chicken stock
3 green onions, chopped
salt and freshly ground pepper to taste
1/2 tsp. chopped mint
1/2 cup whipping cream
mint sprigs for garnish

Place peas, stock, onions, salt and pepper in large saucepan. Bring to a boil. Cover and simmer 5 minutes, or until the peas are just tender. Cool slightly. Puree in food processor or blender. Refrigerate until thoroughly chilled. Stir in chopped mint and cream. Serve in wine glasses. Top each serving with a mint sprig.

Preparation time: 10 minutes
Cooking time: 15 minutes
Servings: 6

Russian Sorrel Soup

An array of colorful condiments embellishes this tangy cold soup.

1 bunch green onions, chopped (white part only)
1 tbs. olive oil
1-1/2 cups chopped sorrel leaves
1 qt. chicken stock
2 eggs
salt and pepper to taste
1 cup sour cream **or** 1/2 cup **each** yogurt and sour cream
condiments: sliced radishes, diced cucumbers, chopped hard-cooked eggs,
    chopped green onion tops

Using a large saucepan, saute onions in oil until limp. Add sorrel and saute 2 minutes. Add stock and bring to a boil. Cover and simmer 5 minutes. Let cool slightly. Beat eggs in food processor or blender. With machine running, gradually pour in the warm sorrel-stock mixture. Puree until blended. Return to the saucepan and cook over very low heat until thickened. **Do not boil.** Stir in sour cream, salt and pepper. Chill. Serve cold in bowls. Top with assorted condiments.

Preparation time: 10 minutes
Cooking time: 10 minutes
Servings: 3 to 4

Summer Cucumber Soup

Serve this refreshing soup in large-bowled wine glasses.

1 large cucumber, peeled
1 cup chicken stock
1/2 tsp. dill weed
1/4 tsp. freshly ground pepper
dash salt
1-1/2 tsp. cornstarch blended with 1 tbs. cold water
2 tbs. chopped chives **or** green onion tops
1 tbs. chopped parsley
2/3 cup yogurt

Halve cucumber lengthwise and scoop out seeds. Chop coarsley. Place in a saucepan the cucumber, chicken stock, dill weed, pepper and salt. Bring to a boil and simmer 5 minutes. Stir in the cornstarch paste and cook until thickened, about 2 minutes. Remove from heat and cool slightly. Puree in food processor or blender with 1 tablespoon of chives and the parsley. Blend in yogurt and chill. Serve in wine glasses or bowls and top with remaining chives.

Preparation time: 5 minutes
Cooking time: 15 minutes
Servings: 4 to 6

Cold Curry Soup

Refresh this spicy soup with a fruity garnish of green grapes and red apples.

2 tbs. butter
2 tsp. curry powder
1 slice ginger root, chopped
2 tbs. flour
3 cups chicken stock
2 egg yolks
1 cup half-and-half
Garnishes: halved green grapes and diced red apples

Melt butter in a saucepan. Stir in curry powder and ginger root. Cook 2 minutes, stirring. Add flour and cook 2 minutes longer. Add stock. Bring to a boil. Simmer 10 minutes. Beat egg yolks until light, then add half-and-half. Stir in part of the hot broth and return to the saucepan. Cook, stirring until thickened. **Do not boil.** Cool and refrigerate. Serve in chilled wine glasses or bowls, garnished with fruit.

Preparation time: 10 minutes
Cooking time: 30 minutes
Servings: 6

Duo Vegetable-Fruit Soup

2 onions, chopped
2 carrots, grated
2 Golden Delicious apples, peeled and diced
1 tbs. butter
1 qt. chicken stock
4 medium tomatoes, peeled, quartered and seeded
2 cloves garlic, minced
salt and freshly ground pepper to taste
3 tbs. dry white wine
sour cream for garnish
chopped pistachios **or** sunflower seeds for garnish

Using a large saucepan or soup pot, saute onions, carrots and apples in butter over medium heat, stirring occasionally until glazed and limp. Add stock, tomatoes and garlic. Cover and simmer for 20 minutes. Let cool slightly. Puree in blender or food processor. Stir in wine. Add salt and pepper to taste. Chill. To serve, garnish with a spoonful of sour cream and chopped pistachios or sunflower seeds.

Preparation time: 10 minutes
Chilling time: 4 hours
Servings: 6

Garden Gazpacho

Summer's sun-ripened tomatoes make this frosty soup superb. Be as lavish as you wish with the condiments.

6 ripe tomatoes, peeled and chopped
2 green onions, chopped
1 inner stalk celery, chopped
1 small cucumber, peeled and chopped
1/2 cup shredded carrot
1-1/2 cups vegetable juice cocktail
1-1/2 cups beef stock

2 tbs. vinegar
1 tbs. fruity olive oil
1/2 tsp. salt
freshly ground pepper to taste
2 tsp. fresh chopped basil **or**
   1/2 tsp. dried basil
1 clove garlic, minced

condiments: diced avocado, lime wedges, pistachios, roasted sunflower seeds, butter-toasted croutons, chopped green onions

Place in a large stainless steel or glass bowl the tomatoes, onions, celery, cucumber, carrot, vegetable juice cocktail, beef stock, vinegar, olive oil, salt, pepper, basil and garlic. Cover and refrigerate at least 4 hours. Ladle into bowls. Accompany with small condiment dishes, offering as many as desired.

Preparation time: 5 minutes
Cooking time: 10 minutes
Servings: 6

Cold Gazpacho with Grapes

From Spain comes this robust garlic soup punctuated with the sweet fruitiness of grapes.

2 cups chicken stock
1 pint half-and-half
3 cloves garlic, minced
3 egg yolks
2/3 cup seedless grapes

In a large saucepan heat together the stock, cream and garlic until steaming. In a small bowl beat egg yolks until light. Blend part of the stock mixture into the yolks. Return yolk mixture to the saucepan. Cook, stirring, over very low heat, until soup is slightly thickened. Refrigerate until chilled. Serve in small soup bowls and scatter a half dozen grapes over each serving.

Strictly Vegetable Soups

The wonderful mix of nutritious and flavor-packed vegetables makes a great basis for delicious soups in endless combinations. These soups are often considered accompaniments. For lunch they make good go-alongs with a salad, a sandwich or a plate of cheese and fruit. For dinner, they are tantalizing first courses or they may stand alone at a vegetarian supper.

Most of these soups freeze well. Some, like Black Bean Soup or Orange Carrot Soup, are handy staples to have stashed away in the freezer, ready for quick thawing and spontaneous serving.

Texture, color and flavor are big assets in these vegetable soups. Plus the condiments lend a special flourish. Remember to have handy some fresh herbs from the garden: basil, tarragon or chives, and some toasty butter-laced French bread croutons, sunflower seeds, pistachios or cashews. A shower of shredded or crumbled cheese can add a special richness. Consider Jarlsberg, Gruyere, shredded dry Jack, Parmesan, Romano or even Feta or Blue.

In planning a menu with these soups, think of complementing their colors and flavors with contrasting salads. Let the Minted Pea Soup precede Chicken Salad in Orange Shells (page 158); African Peanut Soup goes with Salad Santa Fe (page 155); or serve Soupe au Pistou with Pineapple Salad Boats (page 170).

Preparation time: 10 minutes
Cooking time: 10 minutes
Servings: 4

Watercress Soup

Spicy watercress makes a zesty first course soup.

1 onion, chopped
1 tbs. butter
1 potato, diced
2-1/2 cups chicken stock
1/8 tsp. **each** ground nutmeg
    and pepper

1 tbs. **each** cornstarch and cold water,
    mixed into a paste
1 bunch watercress, stems removed
1/2 tsp. salt
1 egg yolk
1/3 cup whipping cream

In a large saucepan saute onion in butter until limp. Add potato, stock, salt, nutmeg and pepper. Cover and simmer 10 minutes, or until tender. Stir in cornstarch paste. Cook until thickened. Let cool slightly. Puree in food processor or blender. Add watercress and blend just until finely minced. Return to the saucepan. Beat egg yolks until light with the cream. Stir eggs and cream into the watercress mixture. Heat, stirring, just until thickened. Ladle into bowls.

Preparation time: 10 minutes
Cooking time: 10 minutes
Servings: 6

Vichyssoise

This classic leek and potato soup is superb hot or cold.

1 bunch leeks, **white part only,** sliced
2 cloves garlic, minced
1 tbs. **each** butter and olive oil
1 qt. chicken stock
4 potatoes, peeled and diced
1/2 tsp. **each** salt and dried tarragon
1/3 cup dry white wine **or** Vermouth
3/4 cup whipping cream
2 tbs. chopped chives **or** parsley for garnish

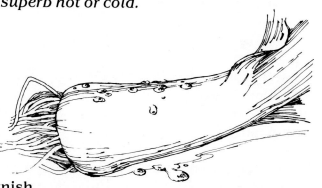

In a large saucepan saute leeks and garlic in butter and oil until limp. Add stock, potatoes, salt and tarragon. Bring to a boil. Cover and simmer 15 to 20 minutes or until very tender. Let cool slightly. Puree in food processor or blender. Blend in wine and cream. Reheat and serve hot or refrigerate and serve chilled. Ladle into bowls. Garnish with chives or parsley.

Preparation time: 5 minutes
Cooking time: 15 minutes
Servings: 4 to 6

Spring Greens Soup

A medley of three different greens gives an appealing flavor in this lightly-spiced broth.

1 tbs. butter
1 bunch green onions, chopped
1 qt. chicken stock
1/4 tsp. salt
1/2 tsp. sugar

2 tsp. soy sauce
2 paper-thin slices fresh ginger root, peeled
1 cup shredded fresh spinach
3/4 cup shredded **or** bite-size chicory
1/2 cup chopped watercress

In a large saucepan melt butter and saute onions until limp. Remove onions and reserve. Pour stock into the pan. Add salt, sugar, soy and ginger root. Bring to a boil. Simmer for 10 minutes. Add spinach, chicory, watercress and the reserved onions. Simmer 2 minutes. Ladle into bowls.

Preparation time: 10 minutes
Cooking time 15 minutes
Serves: 6

Spring Bounty Soup

Herald springtime with this picturesque green and gold soup.

2 tbs. butter
1 leek, **white part only,** chopped
2 cloves garlic, minced
1 carrot, sliced on the diagonal
2 tbs. flour
4 cups chicken stock
1/2 lb. asparagus tips and stems
　peeled and diagonally sliced

1 package (10 ozs.) tiny peas **or**
　fresh shelled green peas
1 dozen pea pods, strings removed and
　cut in half, diagonally
2 tbs. minced parsley
salt and pepper to taste
1/2 tsp. dried tarragon
grated Romano cheese

Melt butter in a large sauce pot. Saute leek, garlic and carrot until tender-crisp. Add flour and saute 2 minutes. Add stock and bring to boil. Add asparagus, peas and pea pods. Simmer 4 to 5 minutes, until asparagus is tender-crisp. Add parsley, season with salt, pepper and tarragon. Ladle into bowls. Sprinkle cheese on top.

Preparation time: 10 minutes
Cooking time: 10 minutes
Servings: 4

Spring Onion-Asparagus Soup

This lush green soup makes a perfect first course for a spring dinner.

3 green onions, chopped
1/4 lb. tree oyster **or** regular
   button mushrooms, chopped
1 tbs. butter
1/2 lb. asparagus

2-1/2 cups chicken stock
2 tsp. cornstarch blended
   with 1 tbs. cold water
1 hard-cooked egg yolk, sieved
   for garnish (optional)

Using a large saucepan, saute onions and mushrooms in butter until glazed, about 3 minutes. Peel ends of asparagus, cut off and reserve the tips. Slice the stems into 1/2-inch lengths. Add stems to sauteed onions and mushrooms. Pour in stock. Bring to a boil. Cover and simmer 5 minutes or until stems are tender. Add asparagus tips, simmer 2 minutes longer. Lift out asparagus tips and reserve for garnish. Place the soup in blender or food processor. Add the cornstarch paste. Puree until smooth. Strain and return to saucepan. Cook until thickened, about 2 minutes. Ladle soup into bowls. Garnish with asparagus tips and sieved egg yolk.

Preparation time: 10 minutes
Cooking time: 10 minutes
Servings: 4 to 6

Creamy Corn Soup

At the height of the corn season, try this delicious soup instead of the usual corn on the cob.

5 ears corn
1 onion, chopped
1 red **or** green pepper, seeded
   and chopped
1 tbs. butter
1 cup **each** chicken stock and milk

2 egg yolks
1 cup half-and-half **or** cream
dash nutmeg
salt and pepper to taste
slivered toasted almonds for garnish

Scrape corn kernels from cobs with a sharp knife, reserving any corn milk. In a large saucepan saute onion and pepper in butter until limp. Add corn, corn milk, chicken stock and milk. Cover and simmer 5 minutes. Puree in food processor or blender. Beat egg yolks. Stir in the cream. Pour part of the corn mixture into the egg and cream mixture. Return to the saucepan with remaining soup mixture. Season with nutmeg, salt and pepper. Heat, stirring. **Do not boil.** Ladle into bowls and garnish with nuts.

Preparation time: 15 minutes
Cooking time: 40 minutes
Servings: 4

Creamy Red Pepper Soup

This sprightly pale-red soup makes an appealing first course. Garnish with a fresh sprig of basil.

3 large sweet red peppers
1 tbs. olive oil
1 onion, chopped
3 cups chicken stock
1 clove garlic, minced

1/2 tsp. paprika
salt and freshly ground black pepper
3 tbs. tomato paste
1/3 cup whipping cream
basil leaves **or** chives, chopped, for garnish

Place peppers on their sides on a sheet of foil. Bake in a 450°F. oven for 20 minutes, turning as the skin blackens. Remove from oven. Place in a paper bag and let set 20 minutes. Peel off skin. Cut peppers in half and remove seeds. Chop coarsely. In a large saucepan heat oil and saute onion until limp. Add chicken stock, peppers, garlic, paprika, salt, pepper and tomato paste. Bring to a boil. Cover and simmer 20 minutes. Let cool slightly. Puree in a food processor or blender. Blend in cream. Heat through or refrigerate. Serve in bowls garnished with basil or chives.

Preparation time: 10 minutes
Cooking time: 20 minutes
Servings: 6

Danish Cauliflower Soup

Let this creamy soup begin a dinner of little Danish meatballs or roast pork with prunes.

1 leek, **white part only, or** small onion, chopped
2 tbs. butter
1 qt. chicken stock
1 lb. cauliflowerettes
salt and freshly ground pepper to taste
1/8 tsp. nutmeg
1/2 cup half-and-half **or** whipping cream
1/2 cup shredded Danish Fontina cheese
1 tbs. minced chives

Using a large saucepan, saute leek in butter until limp. Add stock and cauliflowerettes. Bring to a boil. Cover and simmer 10 to 15 minutes, or until tender. Cool slightly. Puree in a food processor or blender. Return to saucepan. Salt and pepper to taste. Add nutmeg and cream. Heat through. Ladle into bowls. Sprinkle with cheese and chives.

Preparation time: 5 minutes
Cooking time: 20 minutes
Servings: 4

Orange Carrot Soup

Try this delicious soup either hot or cold.

5 carrots, peeled and sliced
1 large onion, peeled and coarsely diced
2 cloves garlic, minced
2 cups chicken stock
1/2 cup orange juice
1/8 tsp. freshly grated nutmeg
salt and freshly ground pepper to taste
1 tsp. grated orange **or** lemon peel
3 tbs. whipping cream **or** sour cream
1/4 cup coarsely chopped pistachios

Place carrots, onion, garlic and stock in a large saucepan. Bring to a boil. Cover and simmer 15 to 20 minutes or until vegetables are tender. Let cool slightly. Puree in food processor or blender. Blend in orange juice, nutmeg, salt, pepper, grated orange peel and cream. Reheat or refrigerate and serve chilled. Ladle into bowls and garnish with pistachios.

Preparation time: 10 minutes
Cooking time: 30 minutes
Servings: 4 to 6

Celery Root Soup

The distinctive flavor of celery root makes a delicious winter soup.

1 onion, chopped
1 stalk celery, chopped
2 tbs. butter
1 celery root (about 1-1/2 lbs.)
1 large potato, peeled and diced

4 cups chicken stock
3/4 cup half-and-half
salt and freshly ground pepper to taste
1/2 tsp. dried tarragon
2 tbs. dry sherry (optional)

Using a large saucepan, saute onion and celery in butter until limp. Peel celery root. Dice and add to pan along with potato. Add stock. Bring to a boil. Cover and simmer 20 to 25 minutes or until the vegetables are tender. Let cool slightly. Puree in a food processor or blender. Add cream, salt and pepper, tarragon and sherry, if desired. Reheat or refrigerate and serve chilled, if desired.

Easy Tomato Soup

The spice of cloves uplifts this fresh-tasting scarlet soup.

1 onion, chopped
1 stalk celery, chopped
1 carrot, grated
2 tbs. butter
1 clove garlic, minced
1 can (6 ozs.) tomato paste
1 bay leaf

4 whole cloves
1 qt. chicken stock
2 tomatoes, peeled and chopped
salt and pepper to taste
2 tsp. chopped fresh basil **or** 1/2 tsp.
   dried basil
sour cream for garnish

Using a large saucepan, saute onion, celery and carrot in butter until limp. Add garlic, tomato paste, bay leaf, cloves and chicken stock. Bring to a boil. Cover and simmer 15 minutes. Remove bay leaf and cloves. Let cool slightly. Puree in food processor or blender with tomatoes. Return to pan. Add salt and pepper and basil. Heat through. Ladle into bowls and garnish with sour cream.

Preparation time: 5 minutes
Cooking time: 20 minutes
Serves: 6

Curried Butternut Soup

Other winter squashes, such as Hubbard, Danish table queen or pumpkin can be substituted for butternut in this spicy soup.

2 tbs. butter
1 onion, chopped
1 leek, **white part only,** chopped
1/2 tsp. curry powder
1/2 tsp. ground allspice
1 butternut squash (about 1 lb.)
   steamed **or** baked

3-1/2 cups chicken stock
salt and pepper to taste
3/4 cup half-and-half
buttered croutons **or** chopped
   red-skinned apple for garnish

Melt butter in a large saucepan. Saute onion and leek until limp. Add curry powder and allspice. Saute 1 minute. Add squash, cut in cubes and chicken stock. Bring to a boil. Cover and simmer 15 minutes. Puree in food processor or blender. Add salt and pepper to taste. Stir in half-and-half. Heat through.

NOTE: For ease in preparation, steam or bake an extra squash at dinnertime for use in making this soup the next day.

Preparation time: 10 minutes
Cooking time: 5 minutes
Servings: 4

Artichoke Soup With Caviar

Here's an elegant first course soup for a party meal. May be served hot or cold.

1 tbs. butter
1 onion, chopped
1 clove garlic, minced
1 tsp. curry powder
2 cups chicken stock
1 package (9 ozs.) frozen
   artichoke hearts, thawed

1 tbs. cornstarch blended with 1 tbs. cold water
2 tbs. white wine
1/2 cup half-and-half **or** whipping cream
salt and pepper to taste
sour cream for garnish
2 tbs. caviar **or** 1/4 cup small cooked shrimp
   for garnish

Using a large saucepan, melt butter over medium-high heat. Saute onion and garlic until glazed. Add curry powder and saute, stirring, for 1 minute. Add chicken stock and artichoke hearts. Bring to a boil. Cover and simmer 5 to 7 minutes or until artichokes are tender. Stir in cornstarch paste and cook until thickened. Remove from heat and puree in food processor or blender. Blend in the wine. Strain. Return to the pan. Add half-and-half. Heat through. Add salt and pepper to taste. Ladle into bowls and garnish with sour cream and caviar or shrimp.

Preparation time: 10 minutes
Cooking time: 20 minutes
Servings: 6

Hungarian Mushroom Soup

Paprika colors and flavors this creamy mushroom soup.

1 small onion, chopped
1 tbs. butter
1/2 lb. mushrooms, sliced
1 tsp. paprika
1 tbs. flour
3 cups beef stock
1 egg yolk
1 cup sour cream

In a large saucepan, saute onion in butter until limp. Add mushrooms and paprika. Saute 2 minutes. Sprinkle with flour and saute 2 minutes longer. Add stock. Bring to a boil. Simmer for 10 minutes. Let cool slightly. Puree in a food processor or blender. In a small bowl beat egg yolk until light and blend in sour cream. Pour some of the mushroom soup into the egg mixture. Return all to the saucepan and heat through, stirring constantly. Ladle into soup bowls.

Preparation time: 10 minutes
Cooking time: 20 minutes
Servings: 6

Sunchoke and Mushroom Bisque

Sunchokes with their rich nutty flavor complement the mushrooms in this creamy soup.

3/4 lb. sunchokes
2 tbs. lemon juice
1 onion, chopped
2 tbs. butter
1/4 lb. mushrooms, sliced
3 cups chicken stock
1 clove garlic, minced

1/2 tsp. dried tarragon
salt and pepper to taste
1/4 cup dry white wine
1/2 cup whipping cream
chopped pistachios, toasted
   slivered almonds **or** sunflower seeds

Peel and dice sunchokes. Place in a bowl of cold water with lemon juice to prevent discoloration. In a large saucepan saute onion in butter until limp. Add mushrooms and saute 1 minute. Add sunchokes, stock, garlic, tarragon, salt and pepper. Cover and simmer 15 to 20 minutes or until sunchokes are tender. Let cool slightly. Puree in food processor or blender. Stir in wine and cream. Return to the saucepan and heat through. Ladle into bowls and garnish with nuts.

Spinach and Mushroom Soup

Preparation time: 10 minutes
Cooking time: 5 minutes
Makes 4 to 6 servings

Either the exotic tree oyster mushrooms or regular button mushrooms can flavor this soup.

1 tbs. butter
4 green onions
1/4 lb. tree oyster **or**
   button mushrooms, sliced
3 cups chicken stock
1 bunch spinach, stems removed
   and leaves coarsely chopped

1 tbs. **each** cornstarch and cold water,
   mixed together
1/2 cup half-and-half **or** yogurt
yogurt **or** sour cream for topping
chopped chives

Using a large saucepan melt butter. Saute onions until limp. Add mushrooms and saute 1 minute. Add stock and bring to a boil. Add spinach and simmer 2 minutes. Stir in cornstarch paste and water. Cook until thickened. Let cool slightly. Puree in food processor or blender. Blend in half-and-half or yogurt. Heat through or serve chilled. Top each bowlful with a spoonful of yogurt or sour cream and chopped chives.

Chinese Mushrooms and Spinach Soup

Preparation time: 10 minutes
Cooking time: 10 minutes
Makes 4 servings

Zestful with ginger, this refreshing light soup makes a delightful starter to an Oriental meal.

4 dried Chinese mushrooms, soaked
1 small carrot
4 cups chicken stock
2 slices ginger root
1 tbs. sesame oil

2 tsp. rice wine **or** dry sherry
2 tsp. light soy sauce
1/2 bunch spinach, stems removed and
    leaves chopped into 2-inch pieces
1 egg, slightly beaten

Soak mushrooms in 1/2 cup water for 30 minutes. Reserve liquid. Slice mushrooms. Peel carrot. Make 4 notches down the sides of the carrot. Slice thinly so each carrot slice resembles a flower. In a large saucepan, bring stock to a boil. Add carrot slices, mushrooms, ginger root, sesame oil, rice wine and soy sauce. Simmer 5 minutes. Add spinach leaves and simmer 1 minute longer. Gradually pour in the beaten egg. Immediately stir to ripple egg into shreds. Remove from heat, and ladle into Chinese soup bowls.

Preparation time: 10 minutes
Cooking time: 20 minutes
Makes 4 servings

Mushroom Potato Stew

A quartet of vegetables lends a lively flavor to this colorful soup. Accompany with a cheese board, fresh green salad and crusty rolls for a complete meal.

2 tbs. butter
1 leek, chopped **or** 3 green onions, chopped
1 carrot, peeled and sliced
2 tbs. flour
3 cups chicken stock
1/2 tsp. dried tarragon

1/2 tsp. salt
1/8 tsp. black pepper
2 large potatoes, peeled and diced
1/2 lb. mushrooms, sliced
1/2 cup half-and-half **or**
   whipping cream

Melt 1 tablespoon butter in a large soup pot. Add leeks and carrots. Saute until limp. Add flour and cook 2 minutes, stirring. Add stock, tarragon, salt, pepper and potatoes. Bring to a boil. Cover and simmer 20 to 15 minutes or until the potatoes are tender. Melt remaining butter in a skillet. Add mushrooms and saute 1 minute. Add sauteed mushrooms and cream to the soup. Heat through.

Mushroom Soup en Croute

Preparation time: 30 minutes
Cooking time: 35 minutes
Makes 4 servings

A golden cap of puff pastry makes an elegant topping for this mushroom soup. Assemble in advance for easy last minute baking.

1 small onion, finely chopped
1 small carrot, shredded
1 inner stalk celery, finely diced
2 tbs. butter
3/4 lb. mushrooms, chopped
2 tbs. flour
3 cups chicken stock
1 clove garlic, peeled and minced
salt and pepper to taste
1/4 tsp. dried thyme
1 cup half-and-half **or** whipping cream
1 package (10 ozs.) frozen puff pastry shells **or** puff pastry sheets
1 egg yolk beaten with 1 tbs. cold water

In a large saucepan, saute onion, carrot and celery in butter until vegetables are barely tender. Add mushrooms and saute 2 minutes longer. Sprinkle with flour. Saute 2 minutes more. Stir in chicken stock, garlic, salt, pepper and thyme. Bring to a boil. Cover and simmer 15 minutes. Add half-and-half or cream. Simmer a few minutes longer. Cool slightly. Puree in food processor or blender until smooth. Refrigerate soup to chill completely. Ladle soup into oven-proof cups or bowls to within 1/2 inch of the top. Roll out puff pastry 1/8-inch thick. Cut into rounds 3/4-inch larger than the diameter of the soup cups. Brush the edges of the pastry with the egg yolk mixture. Place pastry over the soup, egg-side down. Carefully press edges of pastry against the outside edge of the soup cup to form a tight seal. The pastry sould be stretched tightly across the top of the bowl. Chill soups in the freezer for at least 30 minutes for pastry to relax and firm up. Preheat oven to 425°F. Brush pastry with egg yolk. Bake for 15 minutes or until pastry is puffed and brown. Serve immediately. Each guest breaks open his own crust.

Preparation time: 10 minutes
Cooking time: 15 minutes
Makes 4 servings

Soupe Au Pistou

1 qt. chicken stock
1 large boiling potato, peeled and diced
1 carrot, peeled and sliced
1/3 lb. fresh green beans, cut in 1-inch lengths
1 medium zucchini, thinly sliced
1 yellow crookneck squash, thinly sliced
1 leek, **white part only,** cut lengthwise and sliced
1/3 cup freshly shelled peas **or** tiny frozen peas, thawed
2 tomatoes, peeled and chopped
1 tbs. chopped parsley
Basil Parmesan Sauce: see below

    Using a large saucepan, heat stock. Add potatoes, carrots and beans. Simmer 8 minutes. Add zucchini, crookneck and leeks. Simmer 5 minutes longer. Add peas, tomatoes and parsley. Simmer 2 minutes longer. Ladle into soup bowls. Top with a spoonful of Basil Parmesan Sauce.

    BASIL PARMESAN SAUCE: Stir together 3 tablespoons chopped fresh basil, 1/4 cup Parmesan cheese, 1 tablespoon olive oil and 1 clove garlic, minced.

◀ **Mushroom Soup En Croute (page 64)**

Preparation time: 10 minutes
Cooking time: 20 minutes
Makes 6 to 8 servings

Finnish Summer Soup

In Finland it is traditional to celebrate the arrival of the first new vegetables with a warming pot of this mixed-vegetable soup.

1 small cauliflower, cut into flowerettes
2 young carrots, sliced
6 small new red potatoes, quartered
1 small onion, chopped
6 string beans, cut in 1-inch lengths
3/4 cup green peas, fresh **or** frozen
1 dozen pea pods (optional)

2 green onions, chopped
2 cups water
3 cups milk **or** light cream
1 tbs. cornstarch
salt and white pepper to taste
2 tbs. butter
1/4 cup chopped parsley

In a large soup kettle place cauliflower, carrots, potatoes, onion and beans. Add water. Cover and simmer until vegetables are tender, about 15 minutes. Add peas, pea pods and onions and simmer 1 minute longer. Add all but 1/3 cup of the milk. Blend the remaining milk with the cornstarch. Stir cornstarch mixture into the soup. Bring to a boil and cook until thickened. Remove from heat. Season with salt and pepper. Top with butter and parsley.

Preparation time: 10 minutes
Cooking time: 25 minutes
Makes 6 servings

All-Out Vegetable Soup

A good selection of garden vegetables flavors this soup, enriched with the tiny tear-drop-shaped pasta known as orzo.

2 tbs. butter
1 leek, **white part only,** chopped
2 cloves garlic, chopped
1 carrot, diced
1 stalk celery, diced
1 turnip **or** potato, diced
1 **each** zucchini and crookneck squash,
    sliced
1 dozen fresh green beans **or** Italian
    green beans, cut in 1-inch lengths

1/2 cup shelled peas
6 cups chicken stock
3 tbs. orzo **or** other small pasta
2 tbs. **each** chopped basil, parsley
    and chives
Freshly grated Romano **or**
    Parmesan cheese

Melt butter in a large soup pot. Saute leek and garlic until limp. Add carrot, celery, turnip and stock. Bring to a boil and simmer 5 to 7 minutes. Add green beans, peas and pasta. Simmer 5 to 7 minutes longer. Season with mixed herbs. Ladle into bowls and pass cheese.

Warm and Wonderful Full-Meal Soups

What a joy it is to let a soup be the star of the meal. Made in advance, these hearty soups are a boon to the working cook. Simply reheat a potful, toss a green salad and heat some crusty French bread. Set out one or two different kinds of cheese and fruit, and dinner is on the table.

These are great soups for outings: a ski cabin supper, a beach house lunch, or even a wintertime outdoor picnic.

Condiments lend charm to many of these soups. Set out bowls of assorted toppings and let family or guests garnish their own bowlful.

Soup suppers are also a great way to entertain. At the holiday season, invite friends and neighbors for a bountiful and easy party. Good candidates are Hearty Vegetable Veal Soup, Puget Sound Clam Chowder and Mexican Fiesta Soup.

Preparation time: 10 minutes
Cooking time: 40 minutes
Servings: 4 to 6

Danish Celery and Blue Cheese Soup

This makes a beautiful soup for a luncheon with brioche, fresh strawberries or peaches and butter cookies for dessert.

1 leek, **white part only, or**
  onion, chopped
2 celery hearts, cut into 1-inch lengths
2 cloves garlic, minced
2 tbs. butter
1 potato, peeled and sliced
2 sprigs parsley

3 cups chicken stock
1/2 cup heavy cream
2 ozs. Danish blue **or** other blue cheese
salt and pepper to taste
toasted slivered almonds **or** croutons
  for garnish, if desired

Using a large saucepan, saute leek, celery and garlic in butter until limp. Add potato, parsley and stock. Bring to a boil. Cover and simmer 25 to 30 minutes or until the vegetables are tender. Let cool slightly. In a food processor or blender puree mixture with cream and cheese. Season with salt and pepper to taste. Heat through. Ladle into bowls. Garnish with nuts or croutons.

Preparation time: 20 minutes
Cooking time: 30 minutes
Servings: 4

Cheddar Cheese Soup

This golden soup is great for a midwinter supper. Serve by itself or with a cold meat terrine, salad and crusty French bread.

3 green onions, including some green
   tops, chopped
1 stalk celery, chopped
1 carrot, shredded
2 tbs. butter
2 tbs. flour

2 cups chicken stock
1/8 tsp. nutmeg
salt and pepper to taste
1-1/2 cups milk
1 cup (4 ozs.) shredded Cheddar cheese
croutons for garnish, if desired

Using a large saucepan, saute onions, celery and carrot in butter until vegetables are glazed. Add flour and saute 2 minutes, stirring. Add stock, nutmeg, salt and pepper. Bring to a boil. Cover and simmer 15 minutes. Let cool slightly. Puree in food processor or blender. Return to the saucepan. Add milk and heat through. Gradually add the cheese, a handful at a time. Stir until cheese melts before adding the next handful of cheese. Ladle into bowls and garnish with croutons.

Preparation time: 10 minutes
Cooking time: 10 minutes
Servings: 4

Macaunese Cheese Soup

This rich, creamy soup comes from the charming Pousada Sao de Tiago Inn in Macau.

1 tbs. butter
2 green onions, chopped
1 carrot, shredded
1 clove garlic, minced
2 cups chicken stock
1/3 cup dry white wine

4 egg yolks
1 cup half-and-half **or** milk
1/4 cup whipping cream
salt and pepper to taste
1-1/2 cups shredded Gruyere **or** Danish Fontina
croutons for garnish

Using a large saucepan melt butter. Saute onions, carrot and garlic until limp. Add stock and wine and bring to a boil. Beat egg yolks until light. Stir in half-and-half and cream. Mix part of the hot stock into the yolk mixture. Pour yolk mixture into the saucepan. Cook, stirring until thickened. Season with salt and pepper. Reserve 2 tablespoons cheese for garnish. Add remaining cheese a handful at a time, stirring until melted. Heat until soup is thick and creamy.

Preparation time: 10 minutes
Cooking time: 25 minutes
Servings: 4

Danish Potato And Cheese Soup

This creamy soup makes a welcome lunch or supper entree on a blustery day. Other cheese such as Samsoe, Monterey Jack or Gouda may be substituted.

3 potatoes, peeled and diced
3 cups water
1/2 tsp. salt
1 tbs. butter
1 onion, chopped
3/4 tsp. dill seeds, crushed in a mortar

1 tbs. flour
1 cup half-and-half **or** milk
salt and freshly ground pepper
1 cup (4 ozs.) shredded Danish Fontina
2 tbs. chopped chives **or** green onion tops

In a large saucepan simmer potatoes in water with salt until tender, about 15 minutes. In a skillet melt butter. Saute onion with dill seeds, about 5 minutes. Sprinkle with flour. Saute 2 minutes. Add half-and-half. Cook, stirring, until thickened. Add to the potato mixture. Add the cheese slowly, stirring until smooth. Season with salt and pepper. Ladle into bowls. Garnish with chives.

Preparation time: 10 minutes
Cooking time: 50 minutes
Servings: 4 to 6

Cheese-Crusted Onion Soup

Several cheeses, sherry and white wine make this onion soup party-perfect.

4 large onions, thinly sliced
1/4 cup butter
3-1/2 cups beef stock
1/2 cup dry white wine
1/4 cup medium-dry sherry
1 tsp. Worcestershire sauce

1 clove garlic, minced
salt and pepper to taste
1-1/2 cups grated Gruyere **or** Jarlsberg cheese
6 slices toasted and buttered French bread
1/4 cup grated Romano **or** Parmesan cheese

Using a large soup pot, saute onions in butter until golden brown. Cook them slowly, about 20 minutes. Add stock, wine, sherry, Worcestershire, garlic, salt and pepper. Bring to a boil. Simmer 20 minutes. Ladle soup into 4 to 6 ovenproof bowls. Top with the Gruyere or Jarlsberg cheese. Add a slice of toasted French bread and sprinkle with grated Romano Cheese. Bake in a 425°F. oven for 10 minutes until soup is hot and bubbly. Then slip under the broiler to brown the cheese.

Preparation time: 10 minutes
Cooking time: 2 hours
Servings: 6

Black Bean Soup

Top this soup with sour cream and accompany with a trio of condiments. The lime wedges complement its peppery liveliness.

2 cups black beans
2 qts. water
2 stalks celery, chopped
1 onion, chopped
2 tbs. olive oil
3 cloves garlic, minced
1 tsp. salt

1 small red dried pepper, seeds removed
1 tsp. ground coriander
1/4 tsp. ground cloves
1 lb. cooked Polish sausage, sliced
garnishes: sour cream,
cilantro sprigs, lime wedges and shredded
Monterey Jack cheese

In a skillet, saute celery and onion in oil until limp. Place beans, water, garlic, pepper, coriander and cloves in a large saucepan. Bring to a boil. Cover and simmer 1-1/2 to 2 hours or until beans are tender. Add salt. Add sausage and heat through. Ladle into bowls. Top with sour cream. Pass small bowls of cilantro, lime wedges and cheese to garnish the soup.

Preparation time: 15 minutes
Cooking time: 2 hours
Servings: 10

Minestrone

This is a great soup to make in quantity, ready for a snow country weekend. The beans are an extra protein source. If you are lucky enough to have some left over, it freezes beautifully.

1-1/2 cups great northern beans
2 qts. water
1 ham bone with some meat
　　(about 1-1/2 lbs.)
1 onion, chopped
1 stalk celery, chopped
1 carrot, diced
2 cloves garlic, minced
1 can (1 lb., 12 ozs.) Italian plum
　　tomatoes, pureed

2 cups chicken stock
1/2 tsp. **each** dried basil
　　and oregano
1 potato, diced
1 zucchini, sliced
3 tbs. small pasta
salt and pepper to taste
shredded Romano cheese for garnish

Place beans in large soup pot. Add water and bring to a boil. Boil 2 minutes. Remove from heat. Let stand 1 hour. Add ham bone. Boil. Cover and simmer 1 hour or until beans are tender. Remove bone from pot. Let cool. Dice meat and reserve. Discard bone. In a large skillet, saute onion, celery and carrot in oil until limp; add to beans along with garlic, tomato puree, chicken stock, basil and oregano. Cover and simmer 15 minutes. Add potato, zucchini and pasta. Simmer 10 minutes longer. Add salt and pepper to taste. Ladle into bowls. Pass cheese for topping.

Preparation time: 10 minutes
Cooking time: 5 minutes
Servings: 4

Bean Curd With Shredded Pork Soup

This is a delectable soup, typically found throughout China.

4 shittake mushrooms, soaked 30
   minutes and sliced
4 cups beef stock
3 ozs. thinly slivered cooked pork
1/2 tsp. salt
1 tbs. dark soy sauce
1 tsp. rice wine **or** sherry

2 slices ginger root, peeled
1 clove garlic, minced
1 tbs. cornstarch blended with
   2 tbs. cold water
8 ozs. bean curd **or** tofu, cut
   in 1/2-inch pieces
few drops sesame oil

Place the sliced shittake mushrooms and any liquid in a large saucepan. Add stock. Bring to a boil. Add pork and simmer 1 minute. Add salt, soy sauce, wine, ginger root and garlic. Simmer 2 minutes longer. Stir in the cornstarch paste. Cook until thickened. Add tofu. Heat through. Sprinkle with sesame oil. Serve at once.

NOTE: If desired, add 1 cup spinach leaves or 1/2 cup watercress leaves the last minute or two of cooking.

Chinese Mushroom and Spinach Soup (page 62) ▶

Preparation time: 10 minutes
Cooking time: 2 hours
Servings: 6

Bean And Lamb Soup

Leftovers from a leg of lamb make a great starting point for this vegetable-laden soup.

1 cup large white northern beans
4 cups chicken stock
2 cups water
leftover lamb roast bones
1 onion, choppped
1 leek, **white part only,** sliced
1 turnip, diced

1 carrot, diced
2 cloves garlic, minced
salt and pepper to taste
1 tsp. dried oregano
1/2 cup dry red wine
1 tbs. chopped parsley
grated Parmesan cheese for garnish

Place the beans in a large saucepan. Cover with stock and water. Bring to a boil. Reduce heat and simmer 2 minutes. Let stand 1 hour. Add lamb bones, and onion. Cover and simmer 1 hour. Add the leek, turnip, carrot, garlic, salt, pepper, oregano and wine. Cover and simmer for 30 minutes more. Ladle into soup bowls. Garnish with parsley and cheese.

Preparation time: 15 minutes
Cooking time: 2-1/2 hours
Servings: 8

Green Split Pea And Ham Soup

This hearty soup makes a perfect midwinter supper. In Sweden it is a traditional Thursday eve entree.

1-1/2 cups dried green split peas
2 qts. water
1 small onion, chopped
1 stalk celery, chopped
1 bay leaf

1 tbs. chopped parsley
salt and freshly ground pepper to taste
1 cup chopped cooked ham
2 medium carrots, shredded
1 tbs. Dijon-style mustard

Using a large saucepan, place split peas in pan with cold water. Bring to a boil. Cover and let simmer 2 minutes. Remove from heat and let stand 1 hour. Add onion, celery, bay leaf, parsley and ham. Bring to a boil. Cover and let simmer 1-1/2 hours. Add carrots, salt and pepper. Simmer 30 minutes more. Stir in mustard.

Preparation time: 15 minutes
Cooking time: 20 minutes
Servings: 6

Chicken and Shiitake Soup With Vegetables

A melange of vegetables flavors this delectable soup.

6 shiitake mushrooms (dried Chinese
　mushrooms)
1 cup cold water
4 cups chicken stock
2 carrots, sliced
2 leeks, **white part only,** sliced
1 parsnip, sliced

1 turnip, sliced
1-1/2 tbs. **each** cornstarch
　and cold water
1/2 cup spinach leaves
1-1/2 to 2 cups diced cooked chicken
2 tbs. chopped parsley

Soak mushrooms in cold water 15 minutes. Remove mushrooms and chop. Reserve liquid. Bring chicken stock to a boil. Add mushroom liquid, mushrooms, carrots, leeks, parsnip and turnip. Cover and simmer for 15 to 20 minutes or until vegetables are tender. Stir in cornstarch paste. Cook until thickened. Add spinach and chicken. Heat until hot through. Sprinkle with parsley. Ladle into bowls.

Preparation time: 15 minutes
Cooking time: 40 minutes
Servings: 6

Mussel Soup With Saffron

With mussels becoming more available this makes a superb seasonal soup.

3 lbs. mussels **or** small hard-shelled clams
1 cup water
1 cup vermouth **or** dry white wine
1 leek, **white part only,** chopped
1 carrot, shredded
1 stalk celery, chopped
2 tbs. butter

reserved mussel stock
1/2 tsp. saffron
1/2 tsp. dried thyme
1 cup whipping cream
salt and pepper to taste
2 tsp. lemon **or** lime juice

Soak mussels in salted water for 30 minutes. Scrub well under cold running water with a stiff brush. Cut off beards. Put in saucepan with water and vermouth. Steam 3 to 5 minutes or until shells open. Discard unopened mussels. Reserve 2 cups cooking liquid. Remove mussel meat and reserve. In a large saucepan, saute leek, carrot and celery in butter until soft. Add mussel stock, saffron and thyme. Bring to a boil. Cover and simmer 15 minutes. Let cool slightly. Puree in blender or food processor. Return to saucepan. Add cream and mussels. Heat through. Season with salt, pepper and lemon or lime juice.

Preparation time: 10 minutes
Cooking time: 10 minutes
Servings: 6

Spinach and Oyster Bisque

A broiled cream topping adds the finish to this intriguing soup.

1 small bunch (about 3/4 lb.) spinach,
   stems removed
1 tbs. butter
1 clove garlic, minced
1 jar (10 ozs.) small shucked oysters **or**
   10 ozs. fresh shucked oysters
2 cups milk

dash nutmeg
salt and pepper to taste
2 egg yolks
3/4 cup half-and-half
3 tbs. dry sherry **or** Madeira
lightly salted whipped cream for
   topping

Wash spinach under cold running water. Shake dry. Place in a large skillet with butter and garlic. Saute 2 minutes, until bright green. Puree the spinach and oysters in food processor or blender. Pour into a large saucepan, add milk and nutmeg. Heat to simmering. Beat egg yolks until light. Stir in half-and-half. Mix part of the hot oyster mixture into the egg mixture. Then stir into the saucepan with the remaining oyster mixture. Heat through, stirring constantly. If desired, spoon into flame-proof bowls, dollop with whipped cream, and place under a broiler until lightly browned.

Preparation time: 10 minutes
Cooking time: 20 minutes
Servings: 6

Puget Sound Clam Chowder

A favorite soup for the seashore or home, when fresh clams are readily available.

4 strips bacon, diced
1 large onion, chopped
3 medium potatoes, peeled and diced
2 cups clam liquid (part chicken stock
  or water, if desired)
2 tbs. **each** butter and flour

2 cups milk
1/2 cup half-and-half
salt and pepper to taste
1-1/2 cups cooked clam meat
2 hard-cooked eggs, chopped
2 tbs. chopped parsley

Using a large soup pot, saute bacon until crisp. Add onion. Cook until golden brown. Drain off any extra fat. Add potatoes and clam liquid. Bring to a boil. Cover and simmer for 10 to 15 minutes, or until tender. In a small pan, melt butter. Blend in flour. Cook 2 minutes. Add milk and half-and-half. Cook, stirring until thickened. Add to the soup along with clam meat. Salt and pepper to taste. Heat through. Add eggs and parsley. Stir gently. Ladle into bowls.

NOTE: To cook clams: Scrub shells. Cover with water. Steam 2 to 3 minutes until shells open. Discard shells and unopened clams. Save liquid for soup.

Preparation time: 10 minutes
Cooking time: 25 minutes
Servings: 4

Deauville Fish Stew

Fennel lends an anise bite to this easy full-meal soup that originated on the Normandy seacoast.

1 tbs. butter
1 onion, chopped
1 leek, **white part only,** chopped
3 cups chicken stock
1 cup dry white wine **or** vermouth
1 large potato, peeled and cut in
   1/4-inch slices
1 carrot, sliced

1 small bay leaf
1/4 tsp. fennel seeds
3/4 lb. boneless red snapper **or** halibut
4 raw medium shrimp, butterflied
   (optional)
salt and pepper to taste
1 tbs. chopped parsley

Melt butter in a large saucepan. Saute onion and leek, stirring, until soft. Add chicken stock and wine. Bring to a boil. Add potatoes, carrot, bay leaf and fennel seeds. Bring to a boil. Cover and simmer until vegetables are tender, about 15 minutes. Cut fish into 1-inch chunks. Add to the soup, along with shrimp. Cover and simmer about 6 minutes more or until fish flakes when prodded with a fork. Season with salt and pepper. Ladle into bowls. Sprinkle with parsley.

Mexican Fiesta Soup (page 98) ▶

Preparation time: 15 minutes
Cooking time: 35 minutes
Servings: 6

San Francisco Cioppino

1 stalk celery, diced
1 carrot, diced
1 leek, **white part only,** minced
2 green onions, chopped
2 tbs. olive oil
2 cloves garlic, minced
1/2 tsp. **each** dried basil and oregano
1 can (20 ozs.) tomato puree
1 cup clam juice **or** fish stock
1/2 cup dry white wine **or** vermouth

1/2 tsp. salt
1/4 tsp. freshly ground pepper
1 dozen small hard-shelled clams
1 lb. red snapper fillets **or** other
    white fish fillets, cut in 1-inch pieces
1/2 tsp. grated lemon **or** orange peel
2 tbs. minced parsley
1 large Dungeness crab, cooked
    and cracked

In a large saucepan, saute celery, carrot, leek and onions in oil until limp. Add garlic, basil, oregano, tomato puree, clam juice, wine, salt, and pepper. Bring to a boil and simmer 15 minutes. Add clams, fish, lemon or orange peel. Simmer 8 to 10 minutes more or just until fish flakes when prodded with a fork. Add crab and heat through. Sprinkle with parsley. Ladle into bowls. Serve with hot steamy hand towels for wiping fingers.

Preparation time: 15 minutes
Cooking time: 1 hour
Servings: 6

Bouillabaisse

Let the bounty of the fish counter dictate the choice of seafood selection here.

2 tbs. olive oil
1 leek, **white part only,** sliced
1 onion, chopped
2 cups canned Italian plum tomatoes
1 tbs. chopped parsley
1/2 tsp. dried thyme
1/4 tsp. fennel seeds
strip orange peel

pinch saffron
2 cups clam juice
4 cups water
2 lbs. assorted fish: snapper, halibut, bass, **and** shellfish: mussels, shrimp, clams, scallops
chopped parsley

Heat oil in a large soup pot. Add leeks and onion. Saute 5 minutes. Add tomatoes, parsley, thyme, fennel seeds, orange peel, saffron, clam juice and water. Bring to a boil. Cover and simmer 40 minutes. Let cool slightly. Puree in food processor or blender. Return to the soup pot. Bring to a boil and add fish, cut in 1-inch chunks. Add shellfish. Simmer 5 to 8 minutes or until fish flakes when prodded with a fork. Sprinkle with parsley.

Preparation time: 10 minutes
Cooking time: 20 minutes
Servings: 4

Seafood Soup, Italian Style

A splash of liqueur or a few fennel seeds lend a taste of licorice to this bountiful seafood stew.

1 onion, chopped
1 stalk celery, chopped
1 carrot, chopped
1 clove garlic, minced
1 tbs. olive oil
2 cups fish stock **or** clam juice
1 can (8 ozs.) tomato sauce
1/2 cup **each** water
   and dry white wine

1 tbs. Pernod **or** other anise liqueur
   or fennel seeds
1/2 tsp. grated lemon peel
salt and pepper to taste
1 lb. boneless white fish, cut into chunks
6 small rock clams **or** mussels,
   well-scrubbed (optional)
1 tomato, peeled and chopped
3 tbs. chopped parsley

Using a large saucepan, saute onion, celery, carrot and garlic in oil until limp. Add stock, tomato sauce, wine, wine vinegar, liqueur or seeds and lemon peel. Cover and simmer 10 minutes. Add fish and clams. Simmer 6 to 8 minutes more. Add tomatoes and parsley. Ladle into bowls.

Preparation time 15 minutes
Cooking time: 40 minutes
Servings: 4

Italian Sausage and Zucchini Soup

Serve this hearty soup winter or summer accompanied by garlic-buttered toasted French bread.

4 mild Italian sausages
1 inner stalk celery, diced
3 medium zucchini, thinly sliced
1 small onion, chopped
3 cups beef stock
1 can (8 ozs.) tomato sauce
1/2 tsp. salt
1/4 tsp. freshly ground pepper
2 tsp. fresh chopped basil **or** 1/2 tsp. dried basil
grated Parmesan **or** Romano cheese for garnish

Using a large saucepan, brown sausages on all sides. Pour off almost all of the fat. Add celery, zucchini and onion. Saute 2 minutes, stirring. Add stock, tomato sauce, salt, pepper and basil. Simmer 30 minutes. Lift sausages from the pot and slice 1/2-inch thick. Return to soup pan. Ladle soup into bowls. Pass cheese.

Preparation time: 10 minutes
Cooking time: 20 minutes
Servings: 6

Caldo Verde

This is the traditional Portuguese soup that is always accompanied with a local red wine and crusty peasant bread.

2 large potatoes, peeled and sliced
1-1/2 qts. water
1 tsp salt
1/4 tsp. freshly ground pepper
3 tbs. fruity olive oil
1 lb. spinach, kale **or** leaf lettuce, cut into strips
1/4 lb. linguica, chorizo or other smoked garlic sausage, simmered,
   browned and thinly sliced

In a large saucepan cook potatoes in boiling water with salt and pepper until tender about 15 minutes. Mash with a potato masher. Add oil and spinach. Boil, uncovered for 1 to 2 minutes, or just until crisp tender. Ladle into soup bowls. Top with a few slices of sausage.

Artichoke Soup with Caviar (page 58) ▶

MENU

Artichoke Soup
with Caviar

Beef Wellington

Green Salad

Chocolate Mousse

Preparation time: 15 minutes
Cooking time: 30 minutes
Servings: 6

Swiss Chard and Meatball Soup

This nourishing full-meal soup makes a great family supper for the snow country. Make ahead and freeze, if desired.

Meatballs: see page 97
1 bunch Swiss chard
1 tbs. olive oil
1 onion, chopped
1 carrot, shredded
1 stalk celery, chopped
1 tsp. dried oregano
5 cups beef stock
1 can (6 ozs.) tomato sauce
1/3 cup dry red wine
1 can (8-3/4 ozs.) garbanzo beans
8 cherry tomatoes, halved
salt and pepper to taste
grated Parmesan cheese

Prepare meatballs. Remove white stem portion from Swiss chard. Slice thinly. Chop the leaves separately. Set aside. Use a large soup pot. Heat oil and saute chard stems, onion, carrot and celery until limp. Add oregano, beef stock, tomato sauce, wine and garbanzo beans. Bring to a boil. Cover and simmer 10 minutes. Drop meatballs into the hot broth. Add the chopped chard leaves and tomatoes. Simmer 10 minutes longer. Season with salt and pepper. Ladle into bowls. Pass grated cheese.

MEATBALLS: Place in a mixing bowl 1 pound ground pork (or 1/2 pound **each** ground pork and ground turkey), 1 egg, 3 tablespoons cornstarch, 1/2 teaspoon **each** salt and ground allspice, 1/4 teaspoon freshly ground pepper, 1 clove garlic, minced and 1 tablespoon chopped parsley. Mix well and shape into 1-inch balls.

Preparation time: 15 minutes
Cooking time: 25 minutes
Servings: 6

Mexican Fiesta Soup

For a colorful Mexican lunch or supper, partner this meatball soup with crispy fried tortillas and a pretty fruit platter of pineapple spears, melon crescents and papaya wedges.

Meatballs: see page 99
6 cups beef **or** chicken stock
1 onion, finely chopped
2 carrots, shredded
1 zucchini, thinly sliced
2 tomatoes, peeled and chopped
3 tbs. chopped cilantro
1 crushed red chile pepper, seeded
1 small sweet red pepper, seeded and chopped (optional)
salt and freshly ground pepper to taste
cilantro sprigs for garnish

Prepare meatballs. In a large saucepan, bring stock to a boil. Add onion, carrots, zucchini, tomatoes, cilantro, chile pepper, red pepper and meatballs. Simmer 15 minutes, or until vegetables are tender and meatballs cooked. Salt and pepper. Ladle into bowls. Garnish with cilantro.

MEATBALLS: Mix together 1 pound lean ground beef (**or** 1/2 pound ground beef and 1/2 pound ground turkey), 1 chopped green onion, 1 clove garlic, minced, 1 egg, 1/2 teaspoon **each** salt and ground cumin, 1/4 teaspoon **each** dried oregano and freshly ground pepper. Shape into 1-inch balls.

Preparation time: 20 minutes
Cooking time: 3 hours
Servings: 6

Hot Borsch

Golden brown sausages, boiled potatoes and dark pumpernickel bread turn this soup into a full meal.

2 lbs. beef shanks
1 tsp. salt
1/2 tsp. black pepper
2 cloves garlic, chopped
1 bunch beets, unpeeled, scrubbed well
1 onion, chopped
2 cups red **or** white chopped cabbage
1 carrot, grated
3 tbs. lemon juice
1/3 cup tomato paste
1 lb. Polish sausages
6 small red potatoes, boiled in skins
1/2 cup sour cream
1 tbs. chopped chives **or** green onion tops

In a large saucepan simmer beef shanks, salt, pepper and garlic in water to cover for 1 hour. Add beets (without greens) and simmer until tender, about 1 hour. Remove meat and beets from stock. Set aside to cool slightly. Slip skins from beets. Grate beets coarsely. Add beets, onion, cabbage, carrots, lemon juice and tomato paste to the pot. Simmer 30 minutes more. Pull meat from bones and remove fat and connective tissue. Add meat to soup. Simmer 15 minutes longer for flavors to blend. Let cool. Chill overnight, preferably. Skim off any fat. To serve, puncture sausages and brown well on all sides. Heat soup. Slice sausages and serve along with potatoes, sour cream and chives to accompany soup.

Preparation time: 20 minutes
Cooking time: 2-1/2 hours
Servings: 6

Hearty Vegetable-Veal Soup

Perfect for a cool weather supper, this soup needs only crusty bread, a fruit basket and cheese board for a complete meal.

2 lbs. veal **or** beef shanks
2 qts. water
1 tsp. salt
2 potatoes, peeled and diced
2 carrots, peeled and sliced
1-1/2 cups shredded green cabbage

1 onion, chopped
1 stalk celery, diced
1 can (8 ozs.) tomato sauce
freshly ground black pepper to taste
1/2 tsp. **each** oregano, basil and thyme

Place meat in a large saucepan with water and salt. Bring to a boil. Cover and simmer 2 hours or until meat is very tender. Remove meat and let cool. Cut meat into chunks. Discard bones. Refrigerate meat and stock separately. When chilled, skim fat from broth. In a large saucepan, heat stock to boiling. Add potatoes, carrots, cabbage, onion, celery, tomato sauce, pepper, oregano, basil and thyme. Simmer 15 minutes or until vegetables are tender. Add cooked cut-up meat. Heat through.

Preparation time: 15 minutes
Cooking time: 2-1/4 hours
Servings: 6

Scotch Broth

Barley lends nuggets of substance to this vegetable-laden lamb broth.

2 lbs. meaty lamb bones, such as neck and breast
6 cups beef stock **or** 6 cups water **and** 6 beef bouillon cubes
1/4 cup pearl barley
2 carrots, grated
2 green onions, chopped
1 turnip, chopped
1 tomato, chopped
1 tbs. chopped parsley
salt and pepper to taste

In a large saucepan place the lamb bones, water, bouillon cubes or stock and barley. Bring to a boil. Cover and let simmer for 2 hours, or until meat is tender. Remove bones from broth. Let cool slightly. Remove meat from bones and discard bones. Pull meat into bite-size pieces. Chill broth and remove fat. Bring stock and meat to a boil. Add carrot, onions, turnip and tomato. Let simmer 10 minutes. Add parsley. Season with salt and pepper. Ladle into bowls.

Salads

◀ **Parisian Sausage and Endive Salad (page 167)**

Introduction

Salads are a joy at any meal. Eye-catching, refreshing, tantalizing, and delectable, they lend a sparkle and a light, fresh ambiance to the table. With today's keen interest in healthy living, they take star billing, offering a wealth of vitamins, minerals and fiber to the diet.

A salad may be simple, or complex. Either way, if it is ultra-fresh and handsomely presented, it is a winner. Salads have that great asset of being versatile and variable. They let the cook be creative and innovative. They are fast to assemble and the results can look spectacular.

This worldly selection of salads is drawn from a wealth of international cuisines. It includes old favorites and new creations. The many salad combinations bring glamor and variety to the table along with a host of healthful eating.

Choosing The Right Greens

One of the secrets of really good salads is the proper choice of greens. This handy guide identifies some of the most popular and readily available greens:

Head or Iceberg Lettuce—The most familiar of all the lettuces. It is juicy and sweet in flavor. Look for firm, compact heads with light green leaves. The leaves when separated from the head make convenient cups or containers for potato, fruit, bean or other salads. A favorite when cut in wedges and served with Thousand Island or other similar dressings.

Bibb or Limestone—Small rosettes of green and yellow leaves which are soft and velvety. The flavor is delicate and the leaves have a chewy texture. They make a marvelous addition to green salads. Also, a preferred lettuce for cooking.

Romaine—A large, long, upright lettuce with stiff, dark green outside leaves. The center leaves become a light yellow and are more crisp and tender. A flavorful lettuce which has a combination of sweet and slightly bitter flavors. One of the most popular lettuces used in green salads and a ''must'' for Caesar Salad.

Leaf or Bronze Lettuce—A large spreading lettuce. It resembles Boston lettuce in texture but the soft, tender leaves do not form a rosette. There are different varieties with flat or curly leaves which may be all green, or green with bronze or red tips. Its flavor is delicate and it adds color and texture interest to salads.

Chicory or Curly Endive—Forms a large head with lightly curled, dark green outer leaves with yellow leaves in the center. Its flavor is somewhat bitter.

Belgian Endive—A pale green sprout of the Endive family. The small, pointy heads are imported and are quite expensive, but elegant. Also somewhat bitter.

Escarole—Resembles curly endive, but its leaves are broader and not as curly. They range from dark green to yellow-green in the center. Somewhat bitter flavor.

Spinach—Tender, young leaves lend interesting taste and color to salads. It mixes nicely with other greens, or can be used alone for an all-spinach salad.

Watercress—A small, dark green plant that grows in running water, not in soil. It has a distinctive, peppery taste. Adds flavor and color to salads, and can be a garnish.

Cabbage—Has large, round heads, either red or green. The red will add color as well as texture to your salads. The crinkly-leafed Chinese or Napa cabbage can also be used.

For exciting salads, experiment with different combinations of these salad greens. There are no rules; you get to decide which ones you like best.

Oils and Vinegars

The wide variety of flavored oils and vinegars on the market create many new opportunies for adding that special touch to your salads.

Besides apple cider vinegar, with its delicate fruity flavor and tawny color, there are a trio of wine vinegars: red, white and rosé. Each of these can be embellished with a sprig of tarragon or dill or a clove or two of garlic or some shallots. Sherry wine vinegar offers a pleasing nut-like flavor and the champagne vinegars add a delicate touch.

In addition there are fruit vinegars such as raspberry, cherry and strawberry. These are white wine vinegars with an infusion of fruit. Their shelf life is short and it is wise to refrigerate them.

Rice wine vinegar offers a clear, colorless and much milder flavor than the other vinegars. It is a good choice for dressing a salad when wine is featured prominently in the meal.

The oils offer a great flavor spectrum as well. Vegetable oils, such as safflower, corn, peanut, sunflower and soybean, are light and delicate compared to olive oil with its more distinctive flavor. All oils have a similar caloric content.

Since olive oil is pressed from olives its flavor is usually aromatic, fruity and full-bodied. Olive oils that are designated as virgin oil from the first cold-pressing

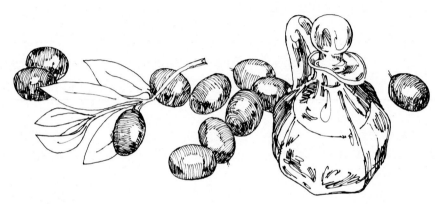

are the highest quality.

In addition, there are the expensive nut oils, such as walnut oil and hazelnut oil. It is wise to purchase salad oil and olive oil in amounts that can be used in a relatively short period of time, because all oils eventually become rancid once they are opened if allowed to stand too long. Store all oils in a cool, dark place, and decant olive oil from a large container into smaller one to prevent the air interacting with it.

Asparagus Mimosa (page 139) ▶

Creating Your Own Salad Dressing The Natural Way

A discreetly blended salad dressing is the key to a choice salad. Whether a basic vinaigrette, a blender or food processor mayonnaise, or a sour cream or yogurt dressing, the basic dressing should interplay to enhance the salad combination.

A well-equipped salad making center has a pepper mill ready for instant grinding, and a supply of garlic, shallots and lemons. A selection of vinegars and oils offer creativity in the kitchen as well.

Cultivate such fresh herbs as parsley, chives, tarragon, mint and basil to lend a superior scent and flavor to dressings.

Timing is important in dressing a salad. Green salads invariably demand last-minute tossing to present them at their peak of crispness. Other salads—vegetable, main dish and fruit combinations—are often more lenient in their rules. For these the dressing often serves as a flavor-packed marinade to penetrate the salad with extra zest. Assemble them in advance to let the flavors mellow as the salad chills.

Vinaigrette Dressing

Here is a basic, versatile dressing to make in quantity. Refrigerate it in a slender wine or vinegar bottle, a good design for shaking and pouring. Use it on green salads, shellfish, sliced tomatoes, raw mushrooms, cooked chilled asparagus, green beans, broccoli, cauliflower, zucchini, beets or other vegetables suited for a vinaigrette treatment. White wine vinegar is recommended for light-colored foods such as mushrooms.

1/2 cup olive oil
1/2 cup salad oil
6 tbs. red **or** white wine vinegar
1 tsp. salt
freshly ground pepper
1 tbs. Dijon-style mustard
3 shallots, peeled and chopped **or** 3 green onions (white part only)

Combine all ingredients in blender container. Cover and blend until smooth. Pour into a bottle and refrigerate. Shake well before using. Makes 1-1/2 cups dressing.

Classic French Dressing

This basic dressing may be varied in numerous ways for countless salads. Make it directly in a salad bowl or shake the ingredients together in a jar or cruet.

2 tbs. red **or** white wine vinegar
1/2 tsp. salt
freshly ground pepper
1 tsp. Dijon-style mustard
6 tbs. salad **or** olive oil

Measure vinegar, salt, pepper, mustard and garlic into a salad bowl. Mix with a fork until blended. Slowly add oil, beating with a fork until the mixture thickens. Or place all ingredients in a jar and shake well until blended. Makes about 1/2 cup.

Variations:

Garlic-flavored Dressing—Add 1 to 2 small clove garlic, minced.

Roquefort or Blue Cheese Dressing—Add 2 to 4 tablespoons crumbled Roquefort or blue cheese to the basic dressing. Mix or shake well.

Lemon Dressing—Substitute lemon juice for the vinegar and add 1/2 teaspoon grated lemon peel.

Fresh Herb Dressing—Add 1-1/2 tablespoons chopped fresh herbs, such as tarragon, basil, or chives, to the basic dressing.

Caper Dressing—Add 2 teaspoons chopped capers and 1/2 teaspoon anchovy paste to the basic dressing.

Lorenzo Dressing—Add 2 tablespoons **each** chili sauce and chopped watercress to the basic dressing.

Poppy Seed Honey Dressing—Place the ingredients for classic French Dressing in a blender container. Add 3 tablespoons honey and blend until smooth. Stir in 1 tablespoon finely chopped green onion and 2 teaspoons poppy seeds. Serve over a citrus fruit salad.

Blender Or Food Processor Mayonnaise

Excellent mayonnaise is swiftly made in a blender or food processor. To create the emulsion it is necessary to add the oil very slowly. If the mayonnaise does not thicken, start again with another egg and slowly blend in the liquified mixture.

1 egg **or** 2 egg yolks
1 tbs. lemon juice
2 tbs. white wine vinegar
1 tsp. sugar
1 tsp. dry mustard
1/2 tsp. salt
1 cup salad oil

Combine all ingredients except oil in blender or food processor, using the steel blade. Process until blended. With the motor at high speed, slowly add the oil in a thin, steady stream through the opening in the cover. Transfer to a covered container and store in the refrigerator. Use within one week. Makes about 1-1/4 cups.

Old-Fashioned Cooked Dressing

For a different flavor use this dressing for potato salad, cole slaw or chicken salad. The consistency is similar to mayonnaise, but it is less expensive and practically fail-proof. A flour-thickened sauce forms the base rather than the high proportion of oil in mayonnaise, so it is lower in calories.

2 tbs. flour
2 tbs. sugar
1 tsp. salt
1 tsp. dry mustard
1/4 tsp. paprika

3/4 cup water
1/4 cup cider vinegar
1 egg, slightly beaten
2 tbs. softened butter

Mix flour, sugar, salt, dry mustard and paprika together in top of a double boiler. Stir in water, vinegar and egg. Cook over hot water, stirring, until sauce is thickened. Remove from heat and stir in butter. Cool, then cover and refrigerate. Makes about 1-1/2 cups.

Thousand Island Dressing

For a quick and easy crisp salad for any season, spoon this all-time favorite over wedges of iceberg lettuce. Top with shredded egg and sprinkle with chopped chives. This salad goes nicely with roast pork or baked salmon.

1/4 cup commercial **or** homemade mayonnaise
1/4 cup sour cream **or** yogurt
3 tbs. bottled chili sauce
1 tbs. lemon juice
dash **each** Worcestershire sauce, Angostura bitters and Tabasco
salt and pepper

Mix mayonnaise, sour cream, chili sauce, lemon juice, Worcestershire, bitters, Tabasco, salt and pepper together well. Chill until serving time. Makes about 3/4 cup, or enough to top 6 wedges of lettuce.

Salade Nicoise (page 164) ▶

Low-Fat Thousand Island Dressing

Approximately half the calories of the original dressing, but with all the flavor.

1/2 cup commercial low-fat mayonnaise
1/3 cup low-fat plain yogurt
1/4 cup cold water
1/4 cup catsup
2 tbs. pickle relish
2 tbs. minced fresh parsley
2 tbs. minced chives **or** green onions

Stir ingredients together until blended. Refrigerate. Makes approximately 1-2/3 cups.

reen Goddess Dressing

amed in honor of the famous actor, George Arliss, when he
ancisco in the play, The Green Goddess. Over the years it
ost popular dressings.

Processor Mayonnaise, page 116

hite wine vinegar

sley, vinegar, garlic, tarragon and anchovies in blender
sley is finely minced. Add sour cream and blend just
rated. Chill, covered, for several hours to blend flavors.

Creamy Blue Cheese Dressing

This sprightly dressing is excellent on chilled, crisp assorted greens such as butter lettuce, romaine and red leaf lettuce. For added spark, mix in hot garlic croutons, diced avocado, marinated artichoke hearts, diced winter pear or cherry tomatoes.

4 ozs. blue cheese (less, if desired)
1/4 cup salad oil
1 tbs. white wine vinegar
1 cup sour cream
3/4 tsp. dry mustard
1/4 tsp. paprika
1/2 tsp. garlic salt
salt and freshly ground pepper

Crumble cheese into a bowl. Blend in oil, vinegar and sour cream with a fork. Stir in mustard, paprika, garlic salt, salt and pepper to taste. Makes about 2 cups.

Yogurt Blue Cheese Dressing

Another dieter's special.

1 cup plain low-fat yogurt
4 ozs. blue-veined **or** Roquefort cheese
3 tbs. wine vinegar
1 clove garlic, minced
1 tsp. salt

    Measure ingredients into blender container or food processor bowl with steel blade. Blend until smooth. If you really don't care about calories you can add a few more small chunks of blue cheese and leave them unblended. Makes approximately 1-1/2 cups.

Low-Calorie Creamy Herb Dressing

A lovely, pale green dressing to perk up any salad, even in the middle of winter. This also makes a great dip for raw vegetables.

5 sprigs watercress
5 sprigs cilantro (Chinese parsley)
1/2 cup **each,** minced green onion and parsley
1 tsp. **each,** dill weed and oregano leaves
1/4 cup white wine vinegar
1 cup buttermilk
1/2 cup **each,** ricotta cheese and low-fat yogurt
salt to taste

Chop watercress and cilantro finely. Combine with onion, parsley, dill and oregano. Pour buttermilk into blender or food processor with steel blade. Add ricotta cheese and yogurt. Blend well, then fold into herb mixture. Add salt to taste. Makes approximately 3-1/2 cups.

Horseradish Cream Dressing

This dressing is excellent served on the Vegetable Salad, page 142. It also makes a good sauce for roast beef or corned beef.

1 large egg yolk
3 tbs. salad oil
1 tbs. fresh lemon juice
2 tsp. Dijon-style mustard
1 tsp. prepared horseradish
1/2 tsp. salt
1/4 tsp. white pepper
2 tbs. olive oil
1/4 cup sour cream

Insert the metal blade into food processor bowl. Add egg yolk, 1 tablespoon salad oil, lemon juice, mustard, horseradish, salt, and pepper. Process to mix. With machine running, gradually add the remaining salad oil and the olive oil. Add sour cream and process just until mixed. Makes approximately 3/4 cup.

Green Salads:
Fresh, Crisp and Nutritious

The popularity of green salads has escalated over the years as the marketplace has become blessed with a variety of different greens and travel has broadened the palates and tastes of Americans.

The green salad plays a role as a first-course starter or in the French manner, as a mid-course, placed between the entree and the dessert. There it makes a delightful interlude and palate cleanser, often paired with one or more cheeses.

When buying greens, choose ones with crisp, fresh leaves. At home, discard discolored or wilted leaves. Store unwashed in a perforated plastic bag in the refrigerator. Before using, wash thoroughly in cold water, drain well on paper towels or in a salad spinner, and place in a plastic bag and refrigerate to crisp.

Iceberg and romaine will keep up to a week—considerably longer than the soft, delicate greens, such as Bibb lettuce.

When ready to assemble a salad, choose a large enough salad bowl so that the greens may be tossed with the dressing with ease. Start with a small amount of dressing. It is easy to add more, adding just enough to coat the greens lightly. Serve at once so the salad is crispy.

A Tossed Green Salad ▶

Caesar Salad

Here's a salad that is fun to mix at the table in front of family or guests.

1 clove garlic, peeled
6 tbs. olive oil
3 tbs. lemon juice
1/2 tsp. salt
1/2 tsp. Worcestershire
1/2 tsp. Dijon-style mustard

freshly grated pepper
1/2 cup freshly grated Parmesan
8 anchovy fillets, chopped (if desired)
1 qt. torn romaine
1 raw egg
1-1/2 cups croutons

Rub cut clove of garlic around inside of the salad bowl. Mix together oil, lemon juice, salt, Worcestershire, mustard, pepper and half the cheese. Add anchovies and romaine. Toss lightly. Break egg onto salad and mix until blended. Sprinkle croutons and remaining cheese over salad. Makes 4 servings.

Green Salad With Warm Chevre Dressing

Chevre is a goat cheese. If it is unavailable use Boursin, a breakfast cheese or natural cream cheese.

6 ozs. mild chevre, such as Montrachet, softened
2/3 cup light olive oil, or as needed
2 to 3 tbs. chopped fresh herbs (a mixture of parsley, chives and tarragon)
1 to 2 tbs. fresh lemon juice
6 cups mixed salad greens (such as watercress and Bibb lettuce)
  or Belgian Endive alone

Heat oven to 375°F. Press cheese into an even layer over the bottom of a small ovenproof dish. Pour enough oil into dish to completely cover cheese. Sprinkle with the herbs. Bake until cheese is melted and soft enough to blend easily with the oil, about 15 minutes. Remove dish from oven. Beat contents with fork, adding lemon juice to taste, until blended. Place greens in individual serving dishes. Pour chevre dressing over greens and serve immediately. Makes 4 servings.

Parsley Salad

This is a great green salad because it is flavorful, and stays delightfully crisp and crunchy.

4 garlic cloves, very finely chopped
8 tbs. olive oil
1-1/2 tbs. wine vinegar (sherry preferred)
salt and freshly ground black pepper
3-1/2 cups parsley, flat and curly mixed if possible, no stems
1/2 cup freshly grated Parmesan cheese

Marinate garlic in olive oil for at least 2 hours before making the salad. Combine it with the vinegar (add more vinegar if you are not using sherry wine vinegar), salt, and pepper. Taste for seasoning. Place parsley in salad bowl. Pour the dressing over parsley and toss. Add cheese and toss again. Makes 4 servings.

Red And Green Cabbage Salad

Make this in advance as it will retain its good crispness when refrigerated up to an hour.

1 small head red cabbage
1 small head green cabbage
3 cloves garlic, peeled and minced
4 flat anchovy fillets, minced

1 tbs. wine vinegar
1/2 cup olive oil
1/2 tsp. **each** salt and pepper
watercress for garnish

Cut cabbages in half. Remove the cores, shred each cabbage separately, and place in separate bowls. Chop garlic and anchovies together to make a paste. In a small bowl, mix together remaining ingredients. Stir in garlic-anchovy paste. (Do not whip or whisk this dressing because you want it to be clear, not like a mayonnaise.) Mix the dressing with each cabbage separately. In a large salad bowl, arrange the red cabbage on the outside and mound the green cabbage in the center. Decorate the edges of the bowl with watercress. Makes 4 to 6 servings.

Russian Coleslaw

Pickles and dill lend a zestful spark to coleslaw.

1 green bell pepper, cut 1/2-inch dice
1/2 head small green cabbage, cut very fine
1 medium carrot, cut in matchstick slices
1 or 2 medium pickles, cut in matchstick
1/2 tsp. salt, or more to taste
watercress

Dressing:
   1/2 cup mayonnaise
   1/2 cup sour cream
   1 tsp. dill weed
   2 tbs. vinegar

Toss pepper, cabbage, carrot, pickles, and salt together in salad bowl. Mix dressing ingredients together and pour over the vegetables. To serve, use a large cooking fork and twirl the salad like spaghetti and place on individual salad plates. Garnish with watercress. Makes 4 servings.

Marinated Mushrooms And Watercress Salad

Offer this spicy salad as a first course, or let it accompany the cheese course.

1 bunch watercress
1 head butter lettuce
1-1/2 lbs. mushrooms
1/4 cup salad oil
1/4 cup olive oil
2 tbs. lemon juice

2 tbs. white wine vinegar
1/2 tsp. salt
1 tsp. Dijon-style mustard
1/4 cup chopped shallots **or** green onions
1/2 tsp. crumbled dried tarragon
1/2 cup cherry tomatoes (optional)

Remove watercress sprigs from stems. Discard stems. Wash sprigs and pat dry. Refrigerate. Wash lettuce leaves well. Pat dry and refrigerate. Slice mushrooms. Place in a large bowl. Blend salad oil, olive oil, lemon juice, vinegar, salt, mustard, shallots, and tarragon together well. Pour over mushrooms. Marinate 1 hour. Add watercress sprigs to mushrooms. Mix lightly. Line a salad bowl with lettuce leaves. Mound mushroom mixture on lettuce leaves. Garnish with cherry tomatoes. Makes 4 servings.

Belgian Endive Salad

Serve this pretty, piquant salad with baked salmon, roast leg of lamb or chicken.

Orange Dressing, see below
1 head romaine
2 heads Belgian endive

1 small red onion
1 jar (6 ozs.) marinated artichoke hearts
2 oranges, thinly sliced

Prepare dressing and set aside. Tear romaine into bite-size pieces. Separate endive leaves. Slice onion and separate into rings. Cut artichoke hearts in half. Combine romaine, endive, onion rings, artichokes, and orange slices in a large salad bowl. Pour dressing over salad ingredients and toss lightly. Makes 4 to 6 servings.

Orange Dressing—Blend together 6 tablespoons olive oil, 3 tablespoons orange juice, 1-1/2 tablespoons lemon juice, 1 teaspoon grated orange peel, 1/4 teaspoon garlic salt and 1/8 teaspoon dry mustard.

Spinach Salad With Apples And Bacon

Either red or gold unpeeled apples lend a bright color accent to this salad.

Spinach Dressing, see below
1 bunch spinach, well washed and dried
4 slices bacon, diced
1 unpeeled apple, cored and diced
1 cup croutons (optional)

Prepare dressing and set aside until needed. Tear spinach into bite-size pieces, discarding the stems. Refrigerate until needed. Using a large frying pan, cook bacon until crisp. Remove with a slotted spoon to paper toweling to drain. Place spinach, bacon and apple in large salad bowl. Pour about 1/4 cup of the dressing over salad. Toss and add more dressing if needed. Add croutons and serve immediately. Refrigerate the remainder of the dressing for another salad. Makes 4 servings.

Spinach Dressing—1/8 cup vinegar, 1/8 cup honey, 1/2 cup salad oil, 3 tbs. Worcestershire, salt and pepper to taste. Mix all of above and reserve until serving time.

Bistro Salad

This superb green salad has just the right interplay of flavors and textures. Consider pairing it with Camembert, Brie or chevre for a combination salad-cheese course.

1 large head butter lettuce
1 bunch watercress, large stems removed
1 avocado
1 red Delicious **or** Winesap apple
1/4 cup chopped toasted filberts, sunflower seeds, walnut halves **or** toasted, slivered almonds
1 tbs. chopped parsley
1 tbs. chives **or** shallots
6 tbs. Vinaigrette Dressing, page 113

Tear lettuce into bite-size pieces. Combine with watercress sprigs in a large salad bowl. Peel and slice avocado. Peel, core, and slice apple. Arrange avocado and apple slices on top of greens. Scatter nuts and herbs over the top. Add dressing and mix lightly. Makes 4 to 6 servings.

Vegetable Salads:
Colorful, Versatile and Delicious

Vegetable salads are a great boon to the hostess-cook since they cleverly integrate the salad course and vegetable into one dish. With such a wealth of vegetables to choose from—raw, cooked and even leftover—the salad combinations are endless.

Another asset of the vegetable salad is its make-ahead quality. They are ideal for a party buffet as they stand up well on the table. Assemble them well in advance and chill them. They usually wait without wilting adding decorative charm to any entertaining occasion.

Select vegetables at their prime, both in freshness and ripeness. Sun-ripened tomatoes far surpass mid-winter's crop. It pays to grow a few plants, in the garden or pots, to enjoy their superior freshly picked flavor in season. To peel them with ease, dip them into boiling water for a few seconds and then plunge them into cold water. Their skins will slip right off.

Enjoy vegetable salads both when entertaining at home or for picnic outings. They travel with ease and marinate en route when packed in a refrigerated ice chest.

Asparagus Vinaigrette Mimosa

Mimosa refers to the yellow spring flowers of France. The yellow yolks of hard-cooked eggs are the "Mimosa" in this pretty salad.

1 to 1-1/2 lbs. asparagus, trimmed
1 tbs. salt
Vinaigrette Dressing, page 113
2 hard-cooked eggs, whites and yolks chopped separately

Bring 2 quarts of water to a rapid boil. Add salt and asparagus. Test in 2 to 3 minutes by tasting one of the spears. Remove asparagus from the water when still crunchy, but cooked. Rinse immediately under cold running water. Drain and chill. Arrange asparagus on a bed of lettuce leaves on a serving dish or on individual salad plates. Pour Vinaigrette Dressing over asparagus. Sprinkle the yolks and then the whites of the eggs **across** the asparagus in two parallel lines. Makes 4 servings.

Leeks Vinaigrette

This makes an excellent summer luncheon dish, or a piquant, classic first course. Clean leeks thoroughly to rinse away their sandy grit.

8 leeks, 3/4-inch in diameter
butter
2 to 3 cups chicken broth **or** water **or** combination of both
salt and freshly ground pepper
Vinaigrette Dressing, page 113

Remove any withered outer leaves from the leeks. Cut off and discard the green upper leaves down to the point where they become pale. Quarter lengthwise to within 1-1/2 inches of the base. Fan out the leaves and wash well under lots of running water. Place cleaned leeks in a buttered saucepan. Pour broth over leeks to cover halfway. Bring broth to boil, cover and reduce to simmer. Cook until tender, approximately 8 to 15 minutes. Remove leeks from liquid. While still warm, cover with Vinaigrette Dressing. Serve lukewarm or chilled. Makes 4 servings.

Broccoli With Rosy Sauce

Serve this attractive salad for a first course. Dark green broccoli and light pink dressing make a striking combination.

1 lb. broccoli
1-1/2 tbs. anchovy paste
1-1/2 tbs. tomato paste
1 clove garlic
3 tbs. parsley sprigs
4 tbs. lemon juice

1/4 cup plain yogurt
1/2 cup commercial **or** homemade mayonnaise
1 bunch Bibb **or** red leaf lettuce, shredded
1-1/2 tbs. finely minced green onion, with tops
8 cherry tomatoes, for garnish

Cut broccoli into attractive pieces. Cook just until crisp-tender. Drain and chill. In blender container or food processor bowl fitted with steel knife, combine anchovy paste, tomato paste, garlic, parsley, lemon juice, yogurt and mayonnaise. Blend well. Mound lettuce on individual plates. Arrange broccoli on lettuce. Spoon dressing attractively over broccoli. Sprinkle onions on top. Garnish with cherry tomatoes. Makes 4 servings.

Layered Vegetable Salad

This vegetable quartet takes on the flavor-packed dressing as it chills.

1 lb. green beans, cooked and cut in 1/2-inch pieces
3 medium carrots, cooked and cut in 1/2-inch pieces
1 pkg. (10 ozs.) frozen peas, cooked **or**
   1-1/4 cups fresh peas, cooked
2 medium beets, cooked, peeled and cut into 1/2-inch cubes
Horseradish Cream Dressing, page 125
2 tbs. minced fresh parsley

Arrange vegetables in attractive layers in a glass salad bowl. Pour dressing over the vegetables. Cover and refrigerate 1 hour. Garnish with parsley before serving. Makes 4 servings.

Pico De Gallo

Meaning "rooster's beak," this Mexican salad goes well with grilled meats or Mexican dishes. The brown-skinned tuber, jicama, was once a novelty in the marketplace. Fortunately it is becoming increasingly available.

1 small head romaine
1 navel orange, peeled and very thinly sliced
1 small cucumber, peeled and sliced
1 small sweet red onion,
  sliced and separated into rings
3/4 cup peeled, chopped jicama

1/2 small red pepper, diced
  (optional)
1/3 cup salad **or** olive oil
3 tbs. white wine vinegar
1/2 tsp. salt
freshly ground pepper

Tear romaine into bite-size pieces and place in salad bowl. Arrange the orange, cucumber, onion, jicama, and pepper on top of romaine. Mix together oil, vinegar, salt and pepper. Pour dressing over salad and mix lightly. Makes 4 to 6 servings.

Tomatoes With Pesto

This zestful, fresh herb dressing enhances summer's vine-ripened tomatoes. It is also superb tossed with hot, well-drained pasta or served over hamburgers or steaks.

1 cup olive oil*
3 cups fresh basil leaves
3 cloves garlic, peeled
1-1/2 tsp. salt

1 cup fresh parsley sprigs
1 cup freshly grated Parmesan cheese
tomatoes

Place oil, basil, garlic and salt in blender container or food processor bowl, fitted with steel blade. Process a few seconds. With motor running, gradually add parsley and Parmesan. Process until mixture reaches a thick consistency. If necessary, add additional parsley or basil. Transfer to a jar with a tight-fitting lid. Chill. At serving time, slice as many tomatoes as desired. Spoon enough dressing over tomatoes to coat lightly. Makes about 1 quart and will keep as long as 2 months.

*or 1/2 cup olive oil and 1/2 cup salad oil

Pepper And Tomato Salad

Typically Italian, this bold salad is a fine companion to lasagne or other pasta and baked Italian sausage.

1 red bell pepper, seeded and chopped
1 green bell pepper, seeded and chopped
1 small, sweet red onion, chopped
1/2 cup chopped parsley
6 tbs. olive oil
3 tbs. white wine vinegar
1/2 tsp. **each** sugar and salt
freshly ground pepper
salad greens
4 large tomatoes, peeled and sliced

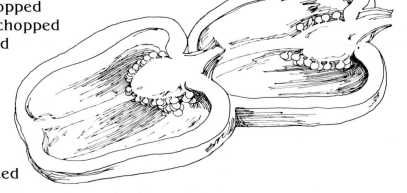

Mix peppers, onion, parsley, oil, vinegar, sugar, salt and pepper in a bowl. Cover and chill 1 hour. Place salad greens on a platter and cover with sliced tomatoes. Spoon marinated peppers and onion over tomato slices. Makes 4 servings.

Guacamole Salad

The renowned guacamole dip becomes a salad when ringed with garnishes.

2 ripe avocados
1/3 cup lemon **or** lime juice
3/4 tsp. salt
1/3 cup finely chopped cilantro
1 clove garlic, minced
1/2 tsp. ground cumin

2 green onions, chopped
lettuce of your choice
1-1/2 cups cherry tomatoes, halved
tortilla chips
radishes and ripe olives

Halve avocados and remove pits. Scoop flesh out into a bowl. Reserve shells. Mash avocado with a fork and mix in lemon juice, salt, cilantro, garlic, cumin and onion. Spoon into avocado shells. Arrange a bed of shredded lettuce on individual salad plates. Place a filled avocado shell in the center of each plate. Surround with cherry tomatoes, tortilla chips, radishes and olives. Makes 4 servings.

As an alternate serving suggestion, spoon guacamole in the center of a platter lined with greens and surround with tomatoes, tortilla chips, radishes and olives.

Tabbouli

Special, finely ground cracked wheat called Bulgur, available in most grocery stores, is needed for this Middle Eastern plumped wheat and vegetable salad. Tabbouli goes well with shish kebab or roast lamb.

1 cup finely ground cracked wheat
1 bunch green onions, chopped
1 cup chopped parsley
1/2 cup lightly packed chopped mint leaves
6 tbs. olive oil
1/3 cup lemon juice

1 tsp. **each** salt and ground allspice
1/4 tsp. ground cumin
freshly ground pepper
1 head romaine
1-1/2 cups cherry tomatoes, halved
1/2 cup Mediterranean-style olives

Place cracked wheat in a sieve and wash under cold running water. Turn into a bowl and add enough water to cover by 1/2 inch. Let stand 1 hour, or until plumped. Drain off any extra liquid. Add onions, parsley and mint to plumped wheat. Mix together oil, lemon juice, salt, allspice, cumin and pepper. Pour dressing over wheat mixture and mix lightly. Line a salad bowl with romaine leaves. Mound salad in the center and ring the outer edge with tomatoes and olives. Makes 4 to 6 servings.

French Potato Salad

For a wholesome picnic spread, serve this hearty salad with sliced sausages, hard-cooked eggs, pickles and olives.

8 to 10 small red boiling potatoes
1/4 cup dry white wine
6 tbs. olive **or** salad oil
2 tbs. white wine vinegar
4 green onions, chopped
1/3 cup chopped parsley
salt and pepper to taste
romaine

Cook potatoes in their skins in boiling salted water until tender. Drain well. Slice. Place in bowl. Pour wine over warm potatoes. Cool. Combine oil, vinegar, onions, parsley, salt and pepper. Pour over potatoes mixing lightly. Cover and chill until serving time. Serve in a bowl lined with romaine. Makes 4 to 6 servings.

Old-Fashioned Potato Salad

A creamy "boiled" dressing gilds diced potatoes and eggs for a great picnic dish. Keep well chilled in an insulated ice chest.

Old-Fashioned Cooked Dressing, page 117
5 large boiling potatoes
4 hard-cooked eggs, sliced
1/2 cup chopped celery
1/2 cup chopped onion
3 tbs. minced parsley
3 tbs. chopped pickles
1 cup cherry tomatoes, halved

Prepare dressing and chill until needed. Scrub potatoes. Do not peel. Cook in boiling water until tender. Peel and dice. Combine potatoes, 2 eggs, celery, onion, parsley and pickle in a salad bowl. Add dressing and mix gently, but thoroughly. Cover and chill. When ready to serve, garnish with remaining sliced eggs and tomatoes. Makes 4 to 6 servings.

French Potato Salad (page 149) ▶
Old-Fashioned Potato Salad (page 150)

Main Dish Salads

Full meal salads are the good cook's friend. These make-ahead salad plates often rely on good leftovers already on hand. Trimmings from a roast or a bird make an inviting appearance on a pretty salad plate.

Main dish salads are good the year around. A warming soup may prelude a salad on a cool day. On a warm evening, a cool entree salad makes a welcome meal.

These main dish salads feature seafood, poultry, beef, and ham. They encompass such favorite old classics as Cobb Salad and newer innovative salads such as Parisian Sausage and Endive. A wealth of international cuisines are represented as well.

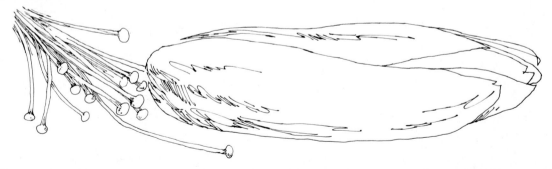

Mexican Beef And Orange Salad

Peppers and oranges enliven this meat salad for a festive summer supper entree.

1-1/2 lbs. rare roast beef **or** steak
2 navel oranges
1 sweet red onion
1 green pepper, seeded
1/3 cup olive oil
1-1/2 tbs. white wine vinegar

1-1/2 tbs. lime **or** lemon juice
1/2 tsp. salt
1/2 tsp. ground cumin **or** Mexican seasoning
salad greens
fresh **or** canned red peppers
1 bunch cilantro (Chinese parsley)

Cut meat into strips. Peel and thinly slice oranges and onion. Slice pepper into strips. Place in a bowl. Mix together oil, vinegar, lime juice, salt and cumin. Pour over meat mixture. Cover and chill at least 2 hours. To serve, arrange greens on a platter. Spoon salad mixture onto greens. Garnish with red peppers and cilantro sprigs. Makes 6 main dish servings.

Note: If desired, cut red peppers, beginning at their tips almost to the stem end, making 5 or 6 strips to resemble flower petals.

Summer Beef Salad

Leftover roast beef makes a fresh appearance as the basis for a cool salad plate.

butter lettuce
1 lb. sliced roast beef
1/3 lb. mushrooms, sliced
1 cup cherry tomatoes, halved
1 cup canned garbanzo beans

1 jar (6 ozs.) marinated artichoke hearts
3 ozs. blue cheese
pitted ripe olives
Tarragon Dressing, see below

Arrange the outer leaves of butter lettuce on 4 dinner plates. Tear the inner leaves and mound in the center of the plate. Overlap the beef slices down the center of each salad. Surround with groups of mushrooms, tomatoes, garbanzo beans, artichoke hearts, a chunk of cheese and olives. Pass Tarragon Dressing. Makes 4 main dish servings.

Tarragon Dressing—Blend together 1/2 cup **each** mayonnaise and sour cream, 2 tablespoons lemon juice, 1/4 teaspoon **each** dry mustard and garlic salt and 1/2 teaspoon dried tarragon.

Salad Santa Fe

Here is a full-meal salad, ideal for a summer supper or guest luncheon.

4 cooked chicken breast halves
5 ozs. Monterey jack cheese
romaine
4 ozs. sliced salami
2 oranges, peeled and thinly sliced

1 avocado, peeled and sliced
sweet red peppers **or** pitted ripe olives
1 dozen tortilla chips
Chile Dressing, see below

Bone chicken breasts and cut meat into strips. Cut cheese into strips. Arrange outer romaine leaves on 4 dinner plates. Finely chop a few inner leaves and place on top. Arrange chicken strips, cheese strips, salami, orange slices, avocado slices, a few peppers and tortilla chips attractively on each plate. Spoon Chile Dressing over tops. Makes 4 main dish servings.

Chile Dressing—Mix together 1/2 cup **each** mayonnaise and sour cream, 2 tablespoons lemon juice, 1/4 teaspoon **each** mustard and garlic salt, 1/2 teaspoon Mexican seasoning or ground cumin and 3 tablespoons canned green chile salsa or chile sauce. Spoon into a bowl and chill. Use as directed.

Tossed Shredded Chicken Salad

Chinese chicken salad makes a captivating supper entree.

1 broiler-fryer chicken (about 2-3/4 lbs.)
Sesame-Soy Dressing, see below
2 cups shredded iceberg lettuce
1 bunch cilantro (Chinese parsley)
1/3 cup diced celery
1/3 cup thinly sliced water chestnuts

2 green onions, cut in 2-inch slivers
1/2 cup cooked small peas
1/4 cup toasted sesame seed **or**
  slivered almonds
fresh pineapple **or** cantaloupe spears

Roast chicken until tender. Chill thoroughly. Remove meat from bones and pull into strips. Place in a salad bowl. Pour Sesame-Soy Dressing over chicken and mix well. Add lettuce, cilantro, celery, water chestnuts, onions, peas and sesame seed. Mix lightly. Spoon onto plates and garnish with 2 or 3 pineapple or melon spears. Makes 4 main dish servings.

Sesame-Soy Dressing—In a small mixing bowl combine 1/2 teaspoon **each** dry mustard and grated lemon peel, 1 tablespoon **each** sugar and honey, 2 tablespoons **each** soy sauce, sesame oil and lemon juice and 1/4 cup salad oil.

Cobb Salad

This stems from the famed Hollywood Brown Derby Restaurant, created by the owner, Bob Cobb. It is one of the few salads which calls for chopping *the lettuce.*

1 small head iceberg lettuce
1/2 head romaine
1 bunch watercress, leaves only
1 large tomato
2 cooked chicken breast halves **or**
   leftover turkey or chicken
1/4 lb. Swiss cheese

1 ripe avocado
2 hard-cooked eggs
4 slices crisp bacon, crumbled
1/4 cup crumbled Roquefort **or** blue cheese
1/4 cup finely chopped parsley
Classic French Dressing, page 114

Chop lettuce and romaine into small pieces using a French knife. Lightly toss chopped lettuces and watercress together in a large salad bowl. Peel, seed and chop tomato. Chop whites and yolks of eggs separately. Chop chicken, cheese, and avocado into small dice. Place tomatoes in a strip across center of greens. Arrange remaining ingredients in separate strips on each side of tomatoes. Sprinkle with parsley. Toss with French Dressing at the table. Makes 4 main dish servings.

Chicken Salad In Orange Shells

1 lemon
2 oranges
2 Golden Delicious apples, unpeeled
3 cups cubed cooked chicken
1/2 cup thinly sliced celery
3/4 cup mayonnaise

2 ozs. Grand Marnier **or** other
orange-flavored liqueur
2 oranges, cut in half, fruit removed
2 ozs. toasted slivered almonds
8 butter lettuce leaves
black olives and watercress

With vegetable peeler, zester or grater, remove peel from the lemon and 2 oranges, being careful not to include any of the white pith. Finely chop peel. Cut oranges into sections. Drain off juice and set aside. Squeeze lemon. Combine lemon juice with orange juice. Core and dice apples. In a large glass or stainless steel bowl, combine chicken, celery apples and peel. Stir in juice mixture. Refrigerate at least one hour. Mix mayonnaise and Grand Mariner. Fold into chicken mixture. Spoon chicken salad into hollowed-out orange shells. Arrange lettuce leaves on 4 individual plates. Place shells in lettuce cups, allowing 1 shells per serving. Sprinkle tops with toasted almonds. Garnish with black olives, reserved orange segments and a sprig of watercress. Makes 4 main dish servings.

Crab Louis

This is a San Francisco classic. It deserves a fume blanc or chardonnay wine and crusty French bread.

4 to 8 butter lettuce leaves
6 cups shredded red leaf **or** iceberg lettuce
1 lb. cooked crabmeat, **or** a mixture of cooked shrimp and crab
Thousand Island Dressing, page 118
2 medium tomatoes, cut in quarters
2 hard-cooked eggs, peeled and quartered
ripe olives and parsley for garnish (optional)

Arrange lettuce leaves on 4 individual plates. Fill with shredded lettuce. Divide the crabmeat among the 4 plates. Spoon dressing over crabmeat. Garnish with eggs and tomatoes. Top with ripe olives and lay a few parsley sprigs at the side. Accompany with more dressing. Makes 4 main dish servings.

Shrimp Stuffed Avocados

San Francisco's famous Green Goddess Dressing uplifts shrimp-stuffed avocados. Consider other fruit and seafood combinations such as papaya or pineapple with crab meat.

romaine **or** butter lettuce
2 avocados
1 lb. shrimp
cherry tomatoes
sliced hard-cooked eggs
pitted ripe olives
Green Goddess Dressing, page 121

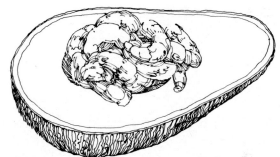

Arrange lettuce on 4 large plates. Peel, halve and seed avocados. Place an avocado half on each plate. Arrange shrimp on top of avocado halves. Garnish salads with tomatoes, egg slices and olives. Pass dressing to spoon over salads. Makes 4 main dish servings.

Aioli Salad Platter

Provencale garlic sauce punctuates a platter of seafood and vegetables.

1/2 lb. fresh green beans*
1 lb. cooked large shrimp
1 egg
1-1/2 tbs. white wine vinegar
1-1/2 tbs. lemon juice
1 tsp. salt

1 tsp. Dijon-style mustard
4 cloves garlic, peeled
1/2 cup salad oil
1/2 cup olive oil
2 cups cherry tomatoes
3/4 lb. fresh mushrooms

Cook green beans and drain well. Shell and devein shrimp. Refrigerate beans and shrimp. Place egg, vinegar, lemon juice, salt, mustard and garlic in blender container or food processor bowl. Blend a few seconds. With motor running, gradually add oil in a slow steady stream. Add enough oil to make a thick mayonnaise. Refrigerate. At serving time, arrange tomatoes, mushrooms, chilled green beans and shrimp on a large platter. Mound sauce in a serving bowl and pass with salad platter. Makes 4 main dish servings.

*or 8- or 9-ounce package frozen artichoke hearts

Fish Salad Mykonos

Cold poached fish is the basis for this main dish salad. In a colorful courtyard taverna on the Greek island of Mykonos this is a gala first course.

1 lb. cold poached turbot **or** sole
1/4 cup olive oil
2 tbs. lemon juice
1 tbs. white wine vinegar
1 tsp. salt
freshly ground pepper
few sprigs mint, chopped

1/3 cup chopped sweet onion
1/4 cup chopped parsley
1/4 cup small cooked shrimp
salad greens
2 tomatoes, cut in wedges
1 jar (6 ozs.) marinated artichoke hearts

Flake fish coarsely into a bowl. Combine oil, lemon juice, vinegar, salt, pepper and mint and pour over fish. Toss in onions, parsley and shrimp. Chill, covered, 1 hour. Serve on salad greens. Garnish with tomatoes and artichoke hearts. Makes 3 to 4 main dish servings.

Note: This salad may also be stuffed into tomatoes which have been cut open like flowers. Garnish with quartered hard-cooked eggs and ripe olives.

Salade Nicoise

Salad "Nee-swaz" is a popular regional dish from Nice, in the south of France.

3 cups cold, cooked green beans
Vinaigrette Dressing, page 113
lettuce leaves for garnishing platter
1 to 2 cans (7 ozs.) white albacore tuna
3 cups French Potato Salad, page 149
4 hard-cooked eggs, peeled and quartered
4 to 8 anchovy fillets
1 cup cherry tomatoes
lemon wedges

Season green beans with 1/4 cup Vinaigrette Dressing. Toss the lettuce leaves with a small amount of vinaigrette. Place them on a chilled serving platter. Arrange remaining ingredients attractively on top of lettuce leaves with the tuna in the middle. Pour about 1/4 cup vinaigrette over the entire salad. Garnish with lemon. Makes 4 main dish servings.

Chef's Salad

The all-time American favorite. And a great way to use leftovers.

1 to 2 bunches lettuce, red-leaf **or** Bibb are good choices
1/4 cup sliced green onions, with some tops
2 cups slivered cooked ham
2 cups slivered cooked chicken **or** turkey
1/4 lb. slivered Swiss **or** American cheese
2 medium tomatoes, cut in wedges
2 hard-cooked eggs, shelled and cut in wedges
3/4 cup Vinaigrette, page 113, **or** dressing of your choice

Tear lettuce into bite-size pieces. Place in a salad bowl. Arrange onions, ham, chicken and cheese in an attractive pattern on top. Place tomatoes and eggs around the edges of the salad bowl. Serve the dressing with the salad. Makes 4 main dish servings.

Ham, Rice And Shellfish Salad

Assemble this salad a day ahead, if desired. Sliced cantaloupe and honeydew make attractive garnishes.

3 cups chilled cooked rice
1 cup cooked crab **or** shrimp
1 cup cooked, slivered ham
1 cup finely chopped celery
2 hard-cooked eggs, finely chopped
1/2 cup chilled cooked peas
1/3 cup chopped parsley
2 tbs. wine vinegar
1/2 cup commercial **or** homemade mayonnaise
salt and pepper to taste

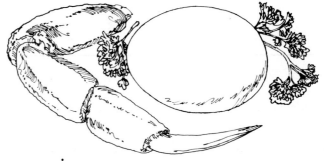

Combine rice, shellfish, ham, celery, eggs, peas and parsley in a large bowl. Mix wine vinegar with mayonnaise. Pour over salad. Taste for seasoning. Chill in refrigerator for a few hours or overnight. Makes 4 main dish servings.

Parisian Sausage And Endive Salad

A "hot and cold" salad, such as this tantalizing version from a Left Bank bistro, is popular in France.

2 or 3 (about 1/2 lb.) mild Italian sausages
2 slices sourdough French bread, cubed
2 tbs. butter
1 clove garlic, minced
1/2 bunch curly endive **or** escarole
1 small bunch romaine

3 slices bacon, diced
1/4 cup olive oil
2 tbs. red wine vinegar
1/2 tsp. salt
1/2 tsp. Dijon-style mustard

Poach sausages in water to cover 20 minutes. Drain and slice diagonally. Saute bread cubes in butter until golden brown. Mix in garlic and set aside. Tear greens into bite-size pieces and place in large salad bowl. Cook bacon until crisp. Drain on paper towel. Reserve drippings. Shake together oil, vinegar, salt and mustard. Pour over greens. Add 3 tablespoons of the reserved bacon drippings. Toss to mix well. Arrange sausage slices on top. Scatter on croutons and bacon. Makes 4 to 6 servings.

Fruit Salads:
Delightful and Refreshing

Fruit salads make eye-catching and refreshing salads or desserts.

Today, thanks to superior storage techniques and swift transportation, fruits are filling the marketplace in greater variety and abundance year-around. Apples, oranges, bananas and pineapple are among the readily available fruits any season. Mangoes, papaya, and kiwi lend a tropical flavor to fruit plates. Grapes from South America are dove-tailing with North American varieties to provide year-around pleasure. Winter pear varieties extend the time span of the summer Bartlett. Strawberries are no longer a spring-through-summer specialty.

With such bounty at hand, fruit salads can be colorful any season.

One tip when cutting such light fruits as bananas, pears or apples is to slice them directly into a bowl of cold water enriched with the juice of one lemon. This citrus bath prevents the cut surface from darkening.

A seasonal fruit medley is a fine way to introduce a brunch or play a starring role at luncheon. Or let a combination fruit salad take on the dessert role.

Capture the best of the season's fruit bounty in delicious, delightful fruit salads to please family or guests.

Pineapple Salad Boats (page 170) ▶

Pineapple Salad Boats

Fresh pineapple shells make handsome containers for a summer luncheon plate or brunch for two.

1 large fresh pineapple
1-1/2 cups seedless grapes
1-1/2 cups watermelon balls
1-1/2 cups strawberries
1/4 cup honey
1/4 cup fresh lime juice
1/2 tsp. grated ginger root

Cut pineapple in half lengthwise, leaving crown of leaves intact. With a grapefruit knife scoop out fruit and dice it, discarding core. Mix pineapple with grapes, watermelon and strawberries. Return to shells. Mix together honey, lime juice and ginger root. Drizzle over fruit. Makes 2 servings.

Fruit Salad And Sherbet

A featured salad plate at a French spa-inn is an artistically arranged pattern of a dozen fruits centered with a trio of sherbets. Accompany with a cheese board and hot croissants.

1 dozen strawberries
4 small bunches seedless grapes
1 **each** orange and grapefruit, cut in segments
1 cup **each** cantaloupe, watermelon and honeydew melon balls
4 half slices or spears fresh pineapple
1 **each** apple and pear, thinly sliced
1 **each** peach and nectarine, sliced
1/2 pint **each** raspberry, lemon and pineapple sherbet
4 mint sprigs
1 pkg. (10 ozs.) frozen raspberries, thawed, pureed and sieved

Arrange on 4 dinner plates a circular pattern of fruits, placing them around the outer edge. Allow space in the center for the sherbets. Place a scoop of each sherbet in the center of each plate. Garnish with mint. Pass raspberry sauce.

Papaya And Avocado Salad

This refreshing salad combination complements fish, seafood or chicken.

2 heads butter lettuce
1 small papaya, peeled and diced
1 avocado, peeled and diced
1/2 cup Vinaigrette Dressing, page 113
1 tbs. lemon juice
1/3 cup chopped macadamia nuts **or** almonds

Tear lettuce into bite-size pieces to make about 4 cups. Place in a salad bowl with papaya and avocado. Toss with dressing. Sprinkle with lemon juice and toss lightly. Scatter nuts over top. Makes 4 servings.

Moroccan Orange And Radish Salad

The bright color combination of the oranges and radishes delights the eye.

3 medium oranges
1 cup thinly sliced red radish
1/4 tsp. ground cumin
salt to taste
1/2 cup freshly squeezed orange juice

Peel and slice oranges, removing all white membrane. On a large plate arrange alternating circles of oranges and radishes. Sprinkle with cumin and salt. Pour orange juice over salad. Chill for 1 hour before serving. Makes 4 servings.

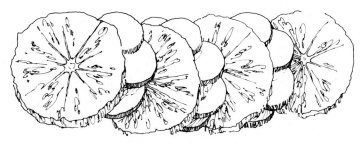

Arabian Nights Fruit Salad

Fresh and dried fruits interplay deliciously in this Moroccan salad.

2 oranges, peeled and diced
1 apple, cored and diced
1/3 cup chopped pitted dates
2 tbs. chopped dried apricots
1 cup freshly squeezed orange juice
2 bananas
1/4 cup chopped toasted almonds

Combine the oranges, apple, bananas, dates and apricots in a large salad bowl. Cover the fruits with the orange juice and taste. If not sweet enough add up to 2 tablespoons granulated sugar. Cover and chill for at least 2 hours. Peel and dice bananas and mix in gently. Serve in individual bowls, topped with the almonds. Makes 4 servings.

Waldorf Salad

Two tones of apples brighten this favorite salad.

2 ripe green or golden apples
1 ripe red apple
juice of 1/2 lemon
1 cup sliced celery
1/2 cup toasted coarsely chopped walnuts
1/2 cup mayonnaise
2 tsp. honey
lettuce leaves for garnish

Core and chop the apples, but do not peel. Place in a bowl and toss with the lemon juice to prevent discoloring. Add celery and walnuts. Mix mayonnaise and honey, or if you wish, use the mayonnaise alone. Stir into apple mixture. Pile salad onto lettuce leaves and serve on individual plates. Makes 4 servings.

Molded Salads:
Make-Ahead Timesavers

Molded salads please the hostess-cook, freeing one for other tasks at the last minute.

A handy hint: A mold comes off more easily if rinsed with chilled water before filling. Be certain to allow enough time for the salad to set thoroughly before unmolding.

To unmold a salad, dip the mold up to the rim in a bowl of hot water for about 4 or 5 seconds. Then place the serving platter on top of the mold, invert mold and give it a firm shake. Lift off mold and refrigerate salad until serving time.

Cranberry Orange Salad (page 178) ▶

Cranberry-Orange Salad

Freshly blended cranberry relish molds nicely into a ruby salad ring to serve with the holiday bird. Fill the ring with orange and avocado slices, if desired.

1 pkg. (12 ozs.) fresh cranberries
2 small unpeeled oranges, quartered and seeded
2 red-skinned apples, quartered and cored
1/2 cup sugar
1 cup orange juice
1 pkg. (6 ozs.) lemon **or** strawberry gelatin
endive **or** butter lettuce

Coarsely chop cranberries, oranges and apples in a blender container or food processor bowl. Transfer to mixing bowl. Stir in sugar. Heat orange juice. Add gelatin and stir until dissolved. Add to cranberry mixture. Turn into a 1-1/2 quart ring mold or bundt pan. Chill until firm. Unmold onto a bed of lettuce. Makes about 8 servings.

Note: For variety, add 1/2 cup chopped pecans to mixture before chilling.

Avocado Mousse

This creamy, light green salad makes a beautiful first course for any special dinner.

2 envelopes unflavored gelatin
1/4 cup cold water
1/4 cup dry sherry
2 cups avocado pieces
2 tbs. chopped green onion
1 cup sour cream

1 cup commercial **or** homemade mayonnaise
1 tsp. salt
1/8 tsp. white pepper
1/4 cup lemon juice
watercress, tomatoes and black olives
   for garnish

Soften gelatin in cold water. Heat over boiling water until melted. Place all ingredients in blender container or food processor bowl. Puree until smooth. Lightly oil 6 individual 1-cup molds. Divide mousse mixture among molds. Cover with plastic wrap and refrigerate until set. Unmold. Garnish with watercress, tomatoes, and black olives. Makes 6 servings.

Molded Orange-Carrot Salad

This classic combination was introduced in the early 1900s. It is also known as "sunshine" or "golden glow."

1 envelope unflavored gelatin
1/2 cup cold orange juice
3/4 cup hot canned pineapple juice
1/4 cup cider vinegar
1/4 cup sugar
1/4 tsp. salt
1 cup drained, crushed pineapple
1/2 cup diced orange sections
1/2 cup shredded raw carrots

Sprinkle gelatin over orange juice in a mixing bowl. Add hot pineapple juice. Stir until gelatin is dissolved. Blend in vinegar, sugar and salt. Refrigerate until partially set. Fold in remaining ingredients and turn into a 4-cup mold. Refrigerate several hours until firm. Unmold onto a chilled plate. Makes 4 to 6 servings.

Sherried Mushroom Mold

This makes a welcome and unusual first course.

1/2 lb. fresh mushrooms
1/4 cup water
2 tbs. fresh lemon juice
1 envelope unflavored gelatin
1/2 cup cold beef bouillon

1-1/2 cups boiling beef bouillon
3 tbs. dry sherry
2 tsp. chopped fresh basil
1 tbs. chopped fresh parsley
salt to taste

Wash mushrooms and remove tough stem ends. Slice. Place in saucepan with water and lemon juice. Cook 2 minutes. Remove and allow to cool in the juices. Soften gelatin in cold beef bouillon. Add boiling bouillon and stir until gelatin is dissolved. Add sherry, basil, parsley and salt. Chill until slightly thickened. Stir in mushrooms. Turn into a 4-cup mold and chill several hours until firm. Slice and serve in butter lettuce cups on individual salad plates. Garnish each with 1 sliced fresh mushroom. Makes 4 servings.

Gazpacho Under Glass

A new look for the Spanish classic. Use it as the centerpiece for your next buffet supper.

2 envelopes unflavored gelatin
1/4 cup cold water
2 cups tomato juice, heated
6 large ripe tomatoes, peeled, seeded and chopped
1 cucumber, peeled and chopped
1 cup thinly sliced celery
1/4 cup finely chopped onion

1/2 cup finely chopped green pepper
4 tbs. olive oil
2 tbs. tarragon vinegar
3 tbs. Tabasco sauce
1/2 tsp. Worcestershire sauce
1 tsp. salt
1/4 tsp. white pepper
salad greens

Soften gelatin in cold water in mixing bowl. Add hot juice and stir until gelatin is dissolved. Refrigerate until slightly thickened. Combine vegetables in large mixing bowl. Mix olive oil, vinegar, Tabasco, Worcestershire, salt and pepper. Stir into vegetables. Combine slightly thickened gelatin and vegetable mixture. Pour into an oiled bundt pan or ring mold. Chill until firm. Unmold onto a bed of greens. Makes 8 to 10 servings.

Borsch Salad With Caviar

Jellied borsch garnished with sour cream and caviar makes a stellar salad companion to veal or pork or a meat terrine.

1 can (15 ozs.) shoestring beets
1 envelope unflavored gelatin
1/2 cup pickle juice
3/4 cup beef stock
1/4 cup chopped sweet onion
1/2 tsp. Worcestershire sauce

1 tbs. prepared horseradish
salt, pepper and dash Tabasco
salad greens
sour cream
black **or** red caviar

Drain juice from beets and measure out 3/4 cup. Soften gelatin in juice. Heat until dissolved. Add pickle juice, beef stock, onion, Worcestershire, horseradish, salt, pepper and Tabasco. Stir in shredded beets. Turn into 6 to 8 small salad molds. Chill until set. Unmold onto a bed of salad greens. Garnish with a spoonful of sour cream topped with caviar. Makes 6 to 8 servings.

Index

Salads continued

Soups

Soups continued

Soups continued

METRIC CONVERSION CHART

Liquid or Dry Measuring Cup (based on an 8 ounce cup)

1/4 cup = 60 ml
1/3 cup = 80 ml
1/2 cup = 125 ml
3/4 cup = 190 ml
1 cup = 250 ml
2 cups = 500 ml

Liquid or Dry Measuring Cup (based on a 10 ounce cup)

1/4 cup = 80 ml
1/3 cup = 100 ml
1/2 cup = 150 ml
3/4 cup = 230 ml
1 cup = 300 ml
2 cups = 600 ml

Liquid or Dry Teaspoon and Tablespoon

1/4 tsp. = 1.5 ml
1/2 tsp. = 3 ml
1 tsp. = 5 ml
3 tsp. = 1 tbs. = 15 ml

Temperatures

°F		°C
200	=	100
250	=	120
275	=	140
300	=	150
325	=	160
350	=	180
375	=	190
400	=	200
425	=	220
450	=	230
475	=	240
500	=	260
550	=	280

Pan Sizes (1 inch = 25 mm)

8-inch pan (round or square) = 200 mm x 200 mm
9-inch pan (round or square) = 225 mm x 225 mm
9 x 5 x 3-inch loaf pan = 225 mm x 125 mm x 75 mm
1/4 inch thickness = 5 mm
1/8 inch thickness = 2.5 mm

Pressure Cooker

100 Kpa = 15 pounds per square inch
70 Kpa = 10 pounds per square inch
35 Kpa = 5 pounds per square inch

Mass

1 ounce = 30 g
4 ounces = 1/4 pound = 125 g
8 ounces = 1/2 pound = 250 g
16 ounces = 1 pound = 500 g
2 pounds = 1 kg

Key   (America uses an 8 ounce cup - Britain uses a 10 ounce cup)

ml = milliliter
l = liter
g = gram
K = Kilo (one thousand)
mm = millimeter
m = milli (a thousandth)
°F = degrees Fahrenheit

°C = degrees Celsius
tsp. = teaspoon
tbs. = tablespoon
Kpa = (pounds pressure per square inch) This configuration is used for pressure cookers only.

Metric equivalents are rounded to conform to existing metric measuring utensils.

ta Fe (page 155)